A Writer's Guide to Self-Publishing and Marketing

Ten-Steps to Success

Barbara Joe-Williams

[AP]

Amani Publishing
P. O. Box 12045
Tallahassee, FL 32317
(850) 264-3341

A company based on faith, hope, and love

Visit our website at: **www.AmaniPublishing.net**

E-mail us at: **AmaniPublishing@aol.com**

ISBN-10: 0978893700
ISBN-13: 9780978893705

LCCN: 2007901008

Cover photo courtesy of: **IStockPhoto.com**

(handwritten) Barbajoewilliams.com
sample contract:
Arthur Page
Dedication
Acknowledge who help
people who
inspired

What people are saying...

I have known Barbara Joe-Williams for almost ten years, and she has been very inspirational in my success as an author. Therefore, I strongly recommend this manual to anyone interested in self-publishing.

Donna R. Austin
Author of "My Christian Diary"
Orlando, Florida

I attended Barbara Joe-Williams first self-publishing workshop, and I was impressed with her delivery and teaching style. This is a wonderful handbook for many aspiring writers.

Doris Maloy
American Business Women's Association
Tallahassee, Florida

Ms. Williams presented a publishing workshop to a large group of educators and other professionals. She provided an easy step-by-step guide on how to self-publish. The response was phenomenal. I have always considered writing novels. Since participating in Ms. Williams' workshop, I have been inspired to resume writing with the intent of self-publishing.

Rhonda Mattox
Bumblebee Enthusiasts Book Club
Little Rock, Arkansas

My sorority invited Barbara Joe-Williams to conduct a self-publishing workshop for our business conference. She is a very motivational speaker who can hold an audience's undivided attention. We would love to have her back!

Judy Williams
Iota Phi Lambda Sorority
Hartford, Connecticut

DEDICATION

*This book is dedicated to my father, the late **Jeffro Joe**.*

Thanks for encouraging me

To become anything that I wanted to be.

Luckily, I finally know what that is.

TABLE OF CONTENTS

INTRODUCTION

Challenges make you discover things about yourself that you never really knew.

Cicely Tyson

Welcome to the world of self-publishing! You purchased this book because you're ready to take the first step in fulfilling your dreams of becoming a published author. Not long ago, I was in your shoes. I had a wonderful idea for a book and after trying the traditional publishing methods, I decided to self-publish. After all, I wrote the book myself so why not publish it myself?

You will find that there are many advantages as well as disadvantages to self-publishing. After reviewing this detailed step-by-step manual, you will be able to make a well informed decision. I warn you now that self-publishing may not be for everyone. However, if it's truly your heart's desire, just do it! I'm happy to show you how.

This ten-step guide shows you how <u>one writer</u> has successfully published several books for herself as well as other aspiring authors. I will guide you through the maze of self-publishing in simple everyday language that will be easy for you to understand and follow. You will be provided with thought provoking open-ended statements, questions, or a checklist at the end of each chapter.

However, it will still require a great deal of motivation and determination to progress from one step to the next. Each big part is broken down into smaller challenges so that the process will not be overwhelming for you. In addition to this valuable information, you will be provided a sample list of contacts for book printers, distributors, and major bookstores along with marketing strategies for increasing your book sales.

WHY I DECIDED TO WRITE
And SELF-PUBLISH

If there's a book you really want to read but it hasn't been written yet, then you must write it.

Toni Morrison

I have been an avid reader all of my life. I especially love reading romance novels. I can trace my love for this genre back to being a teenager during the seventies. My mother loved to read the Harlequin Romance series, and she often bought the magazines featuring true love stories that were really popular during that time. I can remember sneaking to my room to read her books and magazines whenever I had the chance. As I became an adult, I developed a passion for reading love stories along with mysteries and an assorted variety of magazines.

Most of my life has been devoted to reading at least one novel a week. I was especially happy during the nineties when a surge of African-American authors began arriving in the bookstores. From the moment I picked up a copy of *Waiting to Exhale*, by one of my all time favorite authors, Terry McMillan, I was hooked. Reading anything and everything written by an African-American author became a constant desire in my life. I devoured books as one would consume a home cooked Sunday meal, and then revel in the aftertaste with pure satisfaction. At that time, there wasn't a huge selection of African-American authors so I was able to keep up with each book as it arrived fresh off the press. Now we seemingly have a renaissance movement of African-American writers, and I am proud to include myself in the growing number of independently published authors.

After years of reading romance novels, I was finally inspired to write one of my own. I was on Christmas break a couple of years ago from the community college where I was employed as a Reading Assistant when I made a trip to my local bookstore. I wanted to read a positive love story about a long-term married couple that was going through some trials and tribulations that they would be able to overcome. To my surprise, there were very few books available that fit this criterion. In fact, there weren't many romance novels involving married couples at all.

I began to really think about the type of story that I wanted to read when the idea for a romantic storyline suddenly entered my mind. I thought about the concept for days before sharing it with my husband of twenty-four years, and his reaction alone motivated me to bring the novel to fruition. I told him that I'd been thinking about a plot for a romance story for several days, but I wasn't sure if I should try writing it or not. His uninhibited response to me was, "Barbara, as much as you read, you should be able to write something." So with that little bit of inspiration, I prayed that night for God to guide me and the very next morning, I started writing down all my ideas for this story which eventually became titled, *Forgive Us This Day*.

I made a New Year's resolution to complete the book and approximately two months later, I had over two hundred pages to share with my close friends and family. They provided me with positive feedback and the encouragement that I needed to move forward with completing the book. At that point, I'd fallen in love with the writing process and decided to hire an editor, a former colleague who happened to be an English professor, to help me further develop the characters and the plot.

I've always been a good writer, and I'd even been the editor for a few educational newsletters in the past, but I'd never attempted anything of this magnitude.

However, a few months later, I had a finished book and set out to get my manuscript published. I went through the traditional channels of trying to secure an agent and/or a publisher for my book, but to no avail. Finally, after months of frustration, I decided to take my destiny into my own hands and publish the book myself. I loved the story, and I was sure that others would enjoy the novel, too, especially romance readers.

I searched the Internet for several months making contact with other independent publishers and seeking their advice. The few who actually took the time to respond were also very encouraging, which motivated me to keep on pushing towards my goal of becoming a published author. I also researched other famous authors who started out as self-publishers and went on to secure major contracts including: Terry McMillan, Kimberla Lawson Roby, Michael Baisden, E. Lynn Harris, Karen E. Quinones Miller, and John Grisham just to name a few.

Anyway, I decided that I didn't want to spend the next month or the next year of my life mailing out query letters and proposals. I decided to take control of my own destiny by joining the elite ranks of self-published authors. After reading so many books during my lifetime, it seemed like a natural progression for me to become a writer. One thing is for sure, it's a decision that I'll never regret!

I want to write because_____

_____

I want to self-publish because_____

_____

I'm still not sure about publishing because_____

_____

SELF-PUBLISHING FACTS

- The Publishers Marketing Association estimates that there are 73,000 self-publishers in the United States.

- There are approximately 8,000 to 11,000 new publishers entering the field each year, and most of them are independent publishers.

- Of the approximately 2.8 million books in print, 78% of them are from self-publishers.

- From 1997 – 2002, sales increased 21% annually for independent publishers, and they grossed $29.4 billion.

- 81% of the population believes that they have a book inside of them; they just don't know how to get it out.

- Religious book sales, including self help titles, grew by 5.6% in 2004, totaling $1.33 billion.

- The size of the self-publishing industry is rising to an estimated $13 to $17 billion.

- At least 52% of all published books are not sold in bookstores.

- It is predicted that on-line book sales will double between the years 2003 to 2008.

- **Amazon.com** is the leading on-line bookstore for self-published authors.

- The largest growth area in publishing is currently eBooks. In January 2006, eBook sales jumped by over 50%.

Part I

Writing

Barbara Joe-Williams

STEP ONE

DECIDING WHAT TO WRITE

Either write something worth reading or do something worth writing.

Benjamin Franklin

The first decision you will have to make in becoming a self-published author is deciding what to write. I am constantly amazed at the number of people who tell me that they want to write, but they're not sure about how it should be classified. Basically, you only have two choices: fiction or non-fiction. Let's explore the two.

I.   FICTION

Fictional writing is based completely on your imagination. In other words, you're telling lies. Some people don't like to view it that way, but it's the truth. Fictional books are created in your mind even though they may be related to actual experiences in your life or someone else's. If you're not presenting a factual account of what actually happened, then it's purely fiction. It's all right to use real places in fictional writing, although some authors shy away from this. In my debut novel, I used a combination of authentic places and fictitious settings.

Fictional books are classified as novels and usually fall into several categories including mystery, romance, historical romance, contemporary romance, horror, science fiction, paranormal, erotica, etc. For a book to be classified as a novel, it must contain at least 200 pages or a minimum of 50,000 words.

However, most major publishers require at least 300 pages with a minimum of 75,000 words. One of the joys of being a self-publisher is that you don't have to follow the strict industry guidelines.

I chose to write a romance novel because that's what I have the most experience in reading. While I may love a well told mystery story every now and then, my heart will always remain with romance.

A.   Choosing a Voice

If you've decided to write fiction, you have to choose a voice or viewpoint for telling your story. You may want to use the first person voice or the third person voice. With the first person voice, the story is told from the narrator's viewpoint. For example, "It started out as a pleasant day for me. I had a cup of coffee…" You have very limited freedom with this voice because everything is told from one person's perspective, and you can't tell what the other characters are thinking. On the other hand, if you're writing an autobiography, this would be the ideal choice because it allows the reader to experience everything first hand. Another option is to use multiple first person viewpoints for different characters in the story.

If you want to use the third person voice, which is the most popular one, the story is told from the viewpoint of the observer or the writer. For example, "It started out as a pleasant day for Alese. She had a cup of coffee…" This allows you the opportunity to tell a story from various characters perspective's throughout the storyline. You can tell the audience what each character is thinking as the story evolves. This was the easiest way for me to write my first novel. However, the reader becomes the observer and may not feel as involved in the storyline as one would if it was written from the first person perspective. You'll have to make a decision and remain with it throughout the book.

II. NON-FICTION

Non-fictional books are based on reality and research. In other words, you're presenting the facts in the order in which they actually occurred. This is one of the fastest growing book markets today especially with Christian or spiritual writers. You only have to look at Bishop T.D. Jakes, Iyanla Vanzant, Juanita Bynum, or Pastor Joel Olsten to see just how popular this segment has become. Several books fall into this category including how-to books, biographies, self-help books, spiritual guides, etc.

Nonfiction writing can be very lucrative, and you don't have to worry about making up stuff. You can write whatever you want from your point of view or based upon your interpretation. You can tell the whole truth, and nothing but the truth.

If you choose this classification, make sure that you've done your research and can document any facts presented in your manuscript. If your story involves real life characters, you will have to get their permission in writing prior to printing the book. Believe me, once your novel becomes a success, people will look for any possible angle to sue you. I would also suggest that if you're writing about living characters and using their real names, that you consult with an attorney before completing the manuscript.

Did you know that non-fiction typically outsells fiction two to one? The number one non-fiction bestseller for the year 2001 was the *Prayer of Jabez* which exceeded eight million in sales. *Self Matters* was number one on the 2002 list selling only 1,350,000 copies. Robert Kiyosaki and his co-author, Sharon Lechter, sold over one million copies of their self-published book titled, *Rich Dad Poor Dad*, before signing on with a major publisher three years later.

The key to writing non-fiction is to give the people what they want. I'm writing this book because about 80% of the people who have bought my novels want to know how I did it. At every conference or workshop I attend, I'm flooded with questions regarding self-publishing as well as the marketing process.

So in response to the growing demand, I decided to document my experiences into a non-fiction book. As the title states, this is just one writer's way of successful self-publishing. I can't tell you what has worked for others; I just want to share my story about what has worked for me. Hopefully, it will help you become successful, too.

I want to use first person voice.   _____

I want to use third person voice.   _____

I want to write fiction.   _____

I want to write non-fiction.   _____

I'm undecided right now.   _____

STEP TWO

CHOOSING A TITLE

If you haven't dreamed that you will get there, you will not think about ever taking the steps to be there.

Max Robinson

I.   TITLE

Once you have decided whether to write fiction or non-fiction, you need to select a title for your book. It is best to do this before you actually start the writing process because the title will help guide you in preparing and completing your book. The title will help you stay focused on what it is that you wish to accomplish with your book. In other words, you will be writing with a definite purpose in mind.

The title that you choose should be related to your topic and tell exactly what your book is about in as few words as possible. Making a title too long will make it difficult to remember. As a rule of thumb, titles with one to seven words are much easier to recall. When printed, titles should not exceed five lines. Try to use a catchy title that will stay in people minds long after they have read it. Popular songs are usually made into book titles, especially for fictional books.

II.   SUBTITLE

If you need your title to be longer or more detailed than seven words, consider using a subtitle, like I did for this book. This is especially acceptable for non-fictional writing where you're trying to persuade others to buy your specialized book. You want to give the readers as much detail as possible about what they will learn as a result of reading your publication.

Try to start with a catchy title, and then expound on it in the subtitle. Here are some examples of popular non-fiction books with subtitles ( ) that have done well:

A.   Sister CEO
(The Black Woman's Guide to Starting Your Own Business)
Cheryl D. Broussard

B.   Black Titan
(A. G. Gaston & the Making of a Black American Millionaire)
Carol Jenkins & Elizabeth Gardner Hines

C.   The Diva Principle
(Divine Inspiration for Victorious Attitude)
Michelle Hammond

D.   So You Call Yourself a Man?
(A Devotional for Ordinary Men with Extraordinary Potential)
T.D. Jakes

E.   The Debt
(What America Owes to Blacks)
Randall Robinson

III.   RESEARCHING YOUR TITLE

It is important that you have a unique title for your book because a book title <u>cannot</u> be copyrighted. Only the content of a book or song can be copyrighted. This is the reason that song titles can also be used for books over and over again. So there can be ten songs and two hundred books on the market with the same title but the content has to be different.

A good place to start doing a title search is at **Copyright.gov .** This is the official site for copyright registration. This site will show you exactly how many other books have been registered using whatever title you're searching for. It will give you a complete listing of book titles that are currently in print and out of print.

The second best place to do a title search is on-line at Amazon because they are the largest on-line bookstore available. This will give you a current listing of books in print that may have the same title that you have selected.

There is an advantage and a disadvantage to using a title that has been previously used. The advantage is that you will have a popular title that is easy to remember. The disadvantage is that your title will come up with all the other authors when someone does a search for your book. Therefore, my advice would be to take a popular title and change it in some way to make it unique for your publication. For example, for my debut novel, *Forgive Us This Day*, I took a phase from the Bible and changed it to fit my book. While there were several books titled, *Give Us This Day*, there is only one book titled, *Forgive Us This Day*, in the on-line database.

The title of my book is_____

The subtitle of my book is_____

I'm still searching for a title_____

Barbara Joe-Williams

STEP THREE

PREPARING YOURSELF TO WRITE

If one wants to write, one simply has to organize one's life in a mass of little habits.

Graham Greene

Now that you know what to write and you have a title for your manuscript, it's time to start preparing yourself for the writing process. Yes, writing is a process beginning with the title page and ending with the order form at the back of your book. Hopefully, it will be an enjoyable process, but if it's not, then maybe you have chosen the wrong field. Writing should never be forced; it should flow from you as naturally as water from a hot spring.

It does take time, however, to settle into a comfortable writing routine that you can enjoy. But once you get a good writing groove going on, it will be hard for you to put the pen down or turn the computer off.

There is more than one formula or step-by-step process for preparing yourself to write. With time, you'll be able to determine what works best for you. This chapter will help you remove many barriers, discipline yourself, and organize your thoughts and ideas.

I.   FACING YOUR WRITING FEARS

As a beginning writer, you will have writing fears that must be faced early in the game if you want to be a successful author. This is a writing activity that I normally present to my self-publishing workshop attendees. It's a simple, time-limited exercise that encourages participants to really face their writing fears. However, it works just as well with individuals. Please take a few minutes now to face your writing fears.

Simply take out a sheet of blank paper and number it from 1 to 25. Now, set a timer for three-minutes and start jotting down all of your writing fears as fast as you can. Don't stop writing until the timer goes off. If you can't think of anything, then start making up things that you think might hinder you. After all, that's what fictional writers do best (make things up). Just don't worry about how silly it sounds.

At the end of three-minutes, I want you to think about how you felt while you were writing. What you <u>wrote</u> is really not what's important; you should only focus on how you felt as you were trying to complete the activity.

Now, how did you feel? Were you nervous? Did you feel pressured? Did you become agitated? Did you feel your blood pressure rising? Were you anxious? Did you get a headache?

If you answered "yes" to any of the questions above, then you have a taste of what if feels like to be a first time author. This is how every writer feels at the beginning of their writing career when they sit down to immortalize their thoughts for the first time.

There were nights while I was writing my novel when I would become so nervous that I could see my hands actually shaking on the keyboards. But I pressed on and today, all my writing fears have packed up and moved away. Remember that fears come with the territory, but you don't have to entertain them. Just start typing and tell your writing fears to come back later, after you've finished writing your manuscript.

Now that you have listed your writing fears, go back and write a positive response to each negative statement. Save these positive affirmations in a safe place so that you can stay encouraged to meet your writing goals.

If you're still having fears, try deep breathing or physical exercises before starting to type. Once you get past the first chapter, you'll naturally feel more relaxed.

For this next activity, you should be able to list at least three reasons why you want to write.

I want to write because_____

_____

I want to write because_____

_____

I want to write because_____

_____

Now take a few minutes to think about a topic that you feel strongly about. Then set the timer for five-minutes and write all of your thoughts down on this particular subject. This is a great opportunity to test your writing skills. Share this essay with someone that you trust to give you honest feedback regarding your writing style.

II.   WRITING TIPS
Here are some **A – Z** writing tips to help you get started. They have all worked very well for me.

A.   Atmosphere
Creating a peaceful atmosphere is the most essential element to becoming a successful writer capable of meeting publishing deadlines. Having a quiet place to write will help you look forward to writing each day. Some authors like to write in total silence and darkness while others enjoy listening to soft music as they compose their thoughts. Do whatever feels right for you.

B.   Buy
Buy a notebook with dividers to help you get organized. Make a divider for each chapter as you progress and come up with new ideas. Write down all your ideas for the plot twists at the beginning of the notebook. Place them into a logical sequential order and then divide them into chapters. If you're computer literate, this may be done electronically.

C.   Computer
You will need a state-of-the-art computer system equipped with the appropriate software to become a self-publisher. This will be one of your major business investments. You will need enough memory, at least thirty gigabytes, to accommodate any and all graphics related to your book. I would advise you to purchase a laptop computer for mobility because once your book is published, you'll need to travel in order to promote it. I have a Dell Inspiron 5100 with a Pentium-4 processor.

If you're not computer literate, I suggest you take an introductory course at the local vocational school or community college. This will save you money in the long run as well as cut down on your initial start-up costs.

D.   Deadline
Once you start writing, you must set a reasonable deadline for completing your project and stick to it. Think about the length of the book that you want to produce and give yourself ample time for completing it. If you're planning to produce a three hundred page novel, setting a three month deadline will be hard to meet unless you're willing to make some tremendous sacrifices.

E.   Early
Keep a paper and pencil beside your bed for recording those early morning thoughts. Sometime ideas will come to you during the night or through a dream. You don't want to forget them once you're fully awake.

F.   Find

Find yourself a tape recorder to keep in the car for those inspirational ideas you have while driving around during the day. This way, if you sit down to write in the evening, you'll have a transcript to help you get started without having to contemplate where to begin.

G.   Get

Get started using a word processing program with spell check and a thesaurus. Microsoft Word and WordPerfect are the two most popular word processing programs available. You will also need software capable of converting your cover and text file into a portable document format (PDF) file. You'll learn more about this later in Step Seven on Formatting Your Book.

H.   Have

Have a specific schedule for writing each day. Some people write better in the mornings while others find it easier to concentrate after midnight. Try to establish what works best for you at the beginning of the writing process to ensure timely completion of your project.

I.   Imagine

Imagine yourself as a successful writer and communicate with other self-published authors who can help to keep you motivated. Seeing someone else as a success will make your goals seem more realistic, as well as give you something to strive towards. Most bookstores have a special section for local authors and/or self-published writers. Go check out their books and look for their contact information on the inside cover. Usually you'll find an e-mail address or a website for them. Keep trying until someone responds to you.

J.   Journal

Use a daily journal to record your progress. It's easier to keep progressing once you see that some progress has already been made. Keeping a daily journal will also help to clear your thoughts at the end of the day.

K. Kind

Be kind to yourself. Sometimes as a new writer, you will be your own worst critic. Realize that it will take time to develop your writing skills and confidence in your abilities.

L. Love

Write about the type of stories or topics that you love to read, and you'll be a success. If you love mystery novels, then write the best one based on what you've learned from reading them over the years. Just add you own flavor to it and shake it up a bit.

M. Muster

Muster up the strength to write everyday even if it's only for a few minutes or to jot down some key ideas. Every morning that you rise, or the second you arrive home in the evening, you should turn on your computer and don't turn it off until you have typed at least one line into the system. Hopefully, this will motivate you to write even more.

N. New

Remember to put new twists in your plot along the way or add new characters when it's appropriate. Try adding current events into your story to give it more realism and help the reader identify with the time period.

O. Outline

Making a detailed outline prior to beginning your major text will help the writing process go a lot smoother. You don't have to go strictly by the outline, but at least it will provide you some structure while writing your text. Just keep an open mind. Ideas will come to you from every avenue if you let them. Always be receptive to learning different things from other cultures. People want to learn something from reading your book, even if it's a fictional novel, so you can weave in some informing facts and real places.

P. Publish

Keep your publishing goals in mind as you're writing. This will give you a purpose for completing the book within the time limit you have set. Use a desk calendar or planner to chart your goals and keep it in a prominent place where you can view it everyday. Try to have a time block for writing each day even if it's only for an hour.

Q. Questions

Ask yourself the following questions before publishing:

- Who is my target audience?

- How should I price my book?

- Does my plot sound realistic?

- How am I going to promote my book?

- Do I have a niche for marketing my book?

- Are my characters well developed?

- Do I have enough details in the storyline?

- How is my book going to end?

- Am I financially stable enough to self-publish?

- Do I really want to be an entrepreneur?

- Do I normally have problems meeting deadlines?

- Is this something I'm willing to sacrifice for?

- How long will it take me to finish writing my book?

R.   Review
Try not to review your work until you've at least completed the first chapter. This way, you have a better idea about how to start the second chapter. Make sure that you have included all of the pertinent facts so that you can build the next chapter on a firm foundation. Building a solid story is similar to building a brick house. First you lay a concrete foundation and then lay on one brick at a time.

S.   Stop
Stop writing and take a break when you get writer's block. Read something different from what you normally would or watch a television show that you would not usually watch. Get out and meet a new person. You'll be surprised at the new ideas that will come to you even from a simple conversation with a stranger.

T.   Try
Keep trying even if you become frustrated with your work; you can straighten it out with the editor later. Take your time with developing each of the main fictional characters and try to give each one a distinctive voice. If your book is non-fiction, make sure your research is well documented.

U.   Use
Use everything that you know in your fictional writing. For example, if you're an attorney, then place someone in your book in that field or give them a legal issue to resolve. Use every occupation that you're familiar with or have first hand knowledge about. This will give the story a more realistic feel which is exactly what you want.

V.   View
Keep a clear view of how you want the story or book to end. It's okay to add plots and twists to your novel, but make sure that you tie them all up into an airtight conclusion. Your editor will be instrumental in assisting you with this.

W.   Waste

Don't waste too much time with rewriting. This is a common mistake that most new authors make. You keep rewriting the first chapter trying to make it perfect when you should be trying to input as many details as possible so that you can move on to the next one. You will have plenty of time during the editing process to make it a perfect copy.

X.   X-ray

Try to visualize an x-ray of your cover as the book comes together. By the time you're done writing the last word, you want to have the cover file ready for the printer.

Y.   Yourself

Encourage yourself each day to continue writing. Keeping a positive attitude will take you a long way in this business. Reward yourself for meeting each minor deadline with a small token. Share your accomplishment with a close group of friends that will keep you uplifted through their prayers. Also, make sure that you take care of yourself by maintaining healthy eating habits, exercising regularly, and getting lots of rest.

Z.   Zoom

Stay zoomed into your writing style. Don't try to write like anyone else, just write the way that you speak and think. Go ahead and write the synopsis now, before you even start the first chapter. This will help you stay zoomed into what you are supposed to be writing about. In fact, I also suggest that as soon as you complete writing the first chapter, that you write the last chapter. For example, when I wrote my novel, *Forgive Us This Day*, I knew exactly how I wanted it to begin and how I wanted it to end. So immediately after writing the first chapter, I started writing the last chapter. This way, no matter what happened during the course of the book, I knew how it was going to end, and I had my back cover already done.

I hope you will utilize these tips in your writing. The trick to writing a tight story is organization. If you're well organized and have a detailed outline, most of the hard work is already done. I must also say that the Internet is a writer's paradise, and I visit the island as often as possible. You have access to tons of information that it used to take countless hours at the library to find. With just a few clicks, you can have access to the finest entertainment available from any city in the world. Let this be your ticket to the writing circle.

Before you know it, your fingers will be flying across the keyboard trying to keep up with your racing thoughts. Please enjoy your writing adventure; it will be worth the trip!

I enjoyed reading the writing tips.   _____

I plan to use the writing tips.   _____

They weren't helpful to me.   _____

STEP FOUR

EDITING YOUR BOOK

Nothing you write, if you hope to be any good, will ever come out as you first hoped.

Lillian Hellman

I.   FINDING AN EDITOR
There are several places where you should be able to find a qualified editor in your community. You should take your time and conduct a detailed search.

A.   Newspaper or Telephone Directory
The first place to check for an editor would be to look in your local newspaper or the telephone directory under "Editorial Services." You can also call some of your local copy centers in the telephone directory such as FedEx Kinko's or Target Copy because they sometimes have editors working with them on an as needed basis.

B.   College or University System
If you're familiar with the local college/university system, you should call the English department for referrals. At the time I started writing my debut novel, I was working at the community college in the Reading Department so I was familiar with the English and Reading instructors. I spoke with several professors before asking one of them to work with me one-on-one through the editing process.

C.   Referrals
Be sure to ask your editorial candidates for references. You should also check with other local authors for references before making a decision.

There are also many websites on the Internet where you may secure an experienced editor. Remember, with the new technology, you don't have to see the editor face-to-face anymore to have a meaningful exchange. However, I definitely prefer having the convenience of a local contact person.

You can do a **Google.com** search for editors, and then narrow it down to your particular genre. Here are some of the websites I found that offer editorial services. Although I've never used any of these, I did make contact via e-mail or Internet:

- Editavenue.com

- Lmaria23@hotmail.com

- Maxinethompson.com

- Ucanmarkmyword.com

- Writersinthesky.com

II. CHOOSING AN EDITOR
This is a very crucial part of becoming a successful self-publisher. You must find a qualified editor who has experience working with writers and one who is willing to do more than make mere grammatical corrections.

A. Honest Feedback
A good editor will provide you with honest feedback. She will point out the flaws in the storyline or the plots. And in some cases, she might even make suggestions on how to improve the story.

You must be willing to deal with criticism and make the changes accordingly. However, remember that you have the final word and the editor is only making possible suggestions.

B.   Attention to Details

A competent editor pays attention to details that you may have overlooked, such as the timeline, which is very important to the flow of the story. You also need an editor who is knowledgeable regarding your subject matter. One of the key reasons that I chose my editor was because she loved reading romance novels as much as I did. I knew we would be a perfect fit because we had read many of the same books, and she was familiar with the key elements for writing a sellable romance novel.

C.   Accessibility

You want an editor who is going to be accessible to you. If the editor doesn't have time to return a telephone call, how is she going to find time to read your manuscript? Make sure that you have every available access to your editor including her work phone number, home phone number, cellular phone number, and e-mail address. You should establish an open line of communication at the very first meeting. Understand that your editor probably has more than one client, but the two of you should always be able to communicate with each other in a timely manner.

D.   Sharing Yourself

Feeling comfortable sharing yourself with your editor is an instrumental part of being a successful writer and publisher. After all, you two are a team. Both of you should be able to freely express yourselves with one another. It's okay to have different viewpoints because you don't want an editor who agrees with everything that you write.

My editor and I knew each other professionally before I started writing, but through the editing process, we have developed a very close friendship. She is my biggest critic and, yet, she is one of my strongest supporters.

My editor is never afraid to make suggestions because she knows that I will be very receptive to them. In the end, we have the same goal: to produce a believable, well-written, and plot-driven storyline.

One final note regarding choosing an editor: Make sure you're aware of the pay scale prior to making your final selection. Some editors will charge by the word while most of them charge by the page. The average price ranges anywhere from two dollars up to six dollars per typed (double spaced) page. Just be sure that you both make your expectations for each other very clear before any services have been rendered, and you will have a successful working relationship.

III. MAKING REVISIONS & RE-EDITING

Now that your first draft is complete, it's time to make an appointment with the editor. In the past, editing has been done strictly on hardcopy paper. You give the editor a printed copy of your manuscript and she gives it back to you with red or green markings. This is still the preferred method for me. However, with modern day technology, you can e-mail your book to the editor and then she will send it back to you with the editing done in red right on the computer screen. While this is becoming the most conventional way of editing, I've only used this method for revising a couple of pages or a short article.

I gave my editor a hardcopy of my manuscript already formatted for press. We met personally so that I could give her all of the details surrounding the project. Then we agreed on a turnaround time when we could again meet to discuss all of the corrections and suggestions that she would like to make for the manuscript. Most times, I have agreed with her suggestions and made changes accordingly. This is the type of teamwork that will ultimately lead you to success.

Making revisions is probably the most difficult stage of the writing process because it can lead to a great deal of frustration on the writer's part. Having a considerate editor will make the process less irritating for you. I wrote my debut novel in two months, but the editing process took more than four months to complete. I had to do at least three rewrites, but I believe that anything worth having is worth the hard work, so please don't get discouraged.

This is a critical time in the writing process. Just remember that you have the story completed, now you must take the time to fine tune your writing in order to publish the best possible book.

One of my favorite authors, Terry McMillan, stated during an interview years ago that she wrote *Disappearing Acts* in two weeks and *Waiting to Exhale* in two months, but the editing process on each of those projects took her almost an entire year to complete. So, you see, this is a process that should not be rushed by any means. You can write a book as fast as you want, but when it comes to the editing part, you should take it slow. When you're writing fast, it's easy to make mistakes and very hard to catch them. Let the editor do her job.

Editing and re-writing is definitely a challenge especially for a new author. That's why I have a handful of friends who I refer to as my "circle of support." When I'm feeling down and depressed, I call every person on the list and talk to each of them for at least ten minutes. By the time I make it to the last person, I'm usually feeling much better. This is why it's important to always surround yourself with positive people who are going to support your publishing efforts. Sometimes you're going to feel discouraged and completely overwhelmed, just like I did. But I kept pressing on by the grace of God with my strong circle of friends.

By the same token, when I'm flying high and everything is going super well for me, I have a group of people that I can call who will bring me right back to reality. I guess everyone serves a purpose in your life.

IV.   COPYRIGHTING

Copyrighting is one of the major questions that writers interested in self-publishing want to know about. Many authors believe in using the "poor man's copyright" as a way to register their manuscripts. Using this procedure, the author mails a sealed copy of the manuscript to himself as proof of when the document was created.

However, this is not a legalized registration supported by the official copyright office, and may <u>not</u> be honored in a court of law. Go ahead and pay the registration fee if you want to make the manuscript legally yours.

Copyright refers to a form of protection grounded in the U.S. Constitution and granted by law for original works of authorship. Copyright legally covers both published and unpublished manuscripts. Your work is under copyright protection the moment it's created and fixed in a tangible form. However, obtaining a copyright registration number will be beneficial to you if someone illegally duplicates your book and uses it for their personal gain. You will have an official copyright registration number to prove that you were the one who created it first.

A copyright doesn't cover facts, ideas, or discoveries. However, the way that they are expressed in a sequence of words may be copyrighted. For instance, if five other people were also writing a book on self-publishing, we could all use the same facts that I have referenced on page 12. But if anyone else used all the facts in the same format and sequence that I did, then that would be considered plagiarism. As a rule, never copy more three words sequentially from someone else's book. Take the facts presented, and then put them into your own words or unique format for printing.

There are two ways to register for a copyright certificate. You may mail in a copy of your edited manuscript to the copyright office along with the registration form or you may wait and mail in two copies of your published book. Either way you decide, check for the current registration fee before sending in your money. For literary works, you should use Form TX or Short Form TX.

For my first novel, I mailed in the copyright registration twice because after mailing in the original manuscript, I decided to make some significant changes in the story. Once you mail in for a copyright certificate, it's no longer valid if you alter the manuscript. Of course, you're okay if you only have to correct a few minor errors such as changing he to she or you to your.

It may take three to four months to receive your certificate in the mail, but your registration becomes effective on the day that the Copyright Office receives your application. As a general rule, copyright lasts for the lifetime of the author plus an additional 70 years. Here's the contact information for the official Copyright Office:

Library of Congress
Copyright Office
101 Independence Avenue, S.E.
Washington, D.C. 20559-6000
(202) 707-3000
Copyright.gov

Please don't make the mistake of thinking that you can edit your own book. Hire someone who is qualified to help you take your manuscript to the next level. Find an editor who can share your dream and help make it into reality.

I can edit my own book. _____

I will hire an editor. _____

I will register for a copyright. _____

I don't need a copyright registration. _____

Barbara Joe-Williams

Part II

Self-Publishing

Barbara Joe-Williams

STEP FIVE

PUBLISHING OPTIONS

Writing is the only thing that, when I do it, I don't feel as if I should be doing something else.

Gloria Steinem

The majority of people that have asked me for publishing advice are not really sure whether they want to go with an independent publisher, self-publish, or try a traditional publisher. A few years ago, I didn't have any idea that it was even possible for someone to publish their own material. I spent a great deal of time on the Internet researching this new concept with which I had become enthralled. The more I learned about the process, the more I became convinced that this would probably be the best route for me.

There is a general fear that self-published writers are not as credible as major published authors. After all, anyone can write a book and publish it themselves, right? Wrong! Remember, I said that self-publishing is not for everyone. Although I am simplifying the process for you, it still requires a lot of hard work and dedication to publish your own material. Once you've read this complete manual you may decide that self-publishing is not for you. On the other hand, it just might be the answer to your dreams.

While your family and friends are praising you for your self-publishing efforts, the major publishing industry will not embrace you. But that's all right because you're in competition with them, and no one likes competition. It's even difficult for the local press to spotlight authors unless they have received a big contract with a big publishing firm. Don't let that bother you either; just keep pushing your products and making a name for yourself.

You basically have three options when it comes to publishing. If you're determined to see your work in a bound format, you can go the traditional route, self-publish, or try an independent publisher. There are clear cut advantages and disadvantages for each one.

Try to do some detailed research on each avenue of publishing before making your final decision. I'm only giving you my story regarding self-publishing. However, there are many more books and many more stories to be told about this subject. Some self-publishing manuals are over three hundred pages long and contain very technical terminology.

In order to have the whole picture on independent publishers, you need to do some research of your own, and the Internet would be a good place for you to start. There are plenty of websites dedicated to helping you self-publish. I listed several at the end of this book in the reference section.

I.   INDEPENDENT PUBLISHING

Independent publishers are often referred to as "small press" publishers because they're much smaller than the major or traditional publishing houses. They also have much less to offer a new author who's seeking to be published.

Self-published authors may also be considered as fee-based independent publishers or small presses. This means that they charge a fee for their publishing services and cannot pay you an advance for your book.

With an independent publisher, you simply e-mail them the text file, and they do the remainder of the work which may include the editing, formatting, assigning the International Standard Book Number (ISBN), and printing the books. Some of them will even do the copyright registration for you, which may or may not be included in their publishing fees.

Most independent publishers offer package deals which can include a variety of services such as editing, proofreading, cover designing, and marketing strategies. Of course, each package comes with a separate price tag.

Some independent publishers refer to themselves as Print-on-Demand (POD) Publishers because they only print book copies according to the demand or orders that they receive. These publishers include: AuthorHouse, Infinity Publishing, iUniverse, Trafford Publishing, and Xulon Press. They sell most of the books from their website or via on-line bookstores.

Although they don't pay advances like the big publishers, they normally do pay royalties based on the cover price of the book. It's important to mention that while many of these claim that you're self-published by using their services, that's simply not the truth. *If you don't own the ISBN, then you're not self-published.*

A. Advantages of Independent Publishing
- You have some control over your work
- It's easy to work with a small press
- It's less expensive than self-publishing
- It's not very time consuming
- They may provide some promotional materials
- You keep the copyright to your book

B. Disadvantages of Independent Publishing
- You have to pay for publishing services
- You're not paid an advance
- You may be required to pay a set-up fee
- Book copies can be expensive
- They don't provide much marketing help
- You don't own the ISBN

II.   SELF-PUBLISHING

Self-publishing means that you're responsible for making sure that your book gets published. You're also accountable for securing professionals to complete whatever you can't do yourself. This includes, but is not limited to the following: hiring an editor, a cover artist, a website developer, a book printer, and a distributor; as well as financing the whole venture.

By the way, the average start-up cost for a self-publishing business is $5,000 - $10,000. You will need enough working capital to match whatever you expend for your initial start-up costs. This may also be referred to as "maintenance money" or money needed to maintain the business over the course of one year.

Let's examine some of the advantages and disadvantages of this process before moving on:

A.   Advantages
- You're your own boss; you're self-employed
- You keep the copyright to your book
- You gain self-confidence and self-esteem
- You can work full-time or part-time
- You have a good business tax deduction
- You have creative control over your project
- Self-publishing takes less time to produce
- You gain bigger profits
- You can fill a special niche in the market
- You'll have a local advantage

B.   Disadvantages
- Self-publishing is very time consuming
- It can be very costly
- You need a minimum $5,000 start-up
- You need another $5,000 for "working capital"
- It's more difficult to get into major bookstores
- It's harder to get a major book distributor
- You have to contract with outsiders

III.   TRADITIONAL PUBLISHING

Let's look at what the major publishing firms such as Simon & Schuster, Random House, and Dutton have to offer an aspiring writer. Most of the big publishers have admitted that they normally review less than 5% of the manuscripts that they receive each year. If you're one of the lucky few to make it through this limited screening process, they may offer you a writing contract based on producing a certain number of books each year.

In addition, you may be given an advance check based on projected sales or offered up to 10% royalties based on the cover price of your book. At that point you will be assigned an editor. Then, you just have to write the agreed upon number of manuscripts each year and simply turn them in to your editor by the deadline dates.

Now in order to get to this magical point, you have to do some leg work which includes investing a great deal of your time and money. Most of the major publishers will only accept your manuscript from a literary agent. They don't want to deal with individual authors anymore. And merely accepting a copy of your manuscript does not guarantee you anything. However, some major publishing houses, like Kensington, still accept manuscripts without going through an agent and the process is basically the same.

There are a lot of literary agents who specialize in specific genres. You must follow the submission guidelines for each individual agency which normally include submitting a query letter, a book proposal, sample chapters, or sometimes a complete manuscript. Typically, agents earn 15% of the contract price.

A.   Traditional Publishing Steps
Let's examine the steps for the traditional publishing process.

Step One: **Developing a Query Letter**
- a.   A query letter tells the plot of the story
- b.   It describes the storyline's main characters
- c.   It should never be more than one page
- d.   It states the genre, word count, and target market
- e.   It tells something about yourself

Step Two: **Query Letter to Agent and/or Publisher**
- a.   You must send a query letter or e-mail to agent/publisher
- b.   Never send a manuscript without permission from the agent/publisher
- c.   Check the Writer's Market Book for listings

Step Three: **Submission Guidelines (Agent/Publisher)**
- a.   Follow individual guidelines to the letter
- b.   Some will request a synopsis (2-3 pages)
- c.   They may also ask for the first, second and/or third chapters of manuscript and a self-addressed stamped envelope (SASE)
- d.   Some may request the entire manuscript
- e.   Send Priority Mail with delivery confirmation
- f.   Do not call them to follow-up; wait for them to contact you

Step Four: **Acceptance or Rejection?**
- a.   It may take three months (maybe longer) for a reply
- b.   If the manuscript is rejected, you can keep trying or self-publish
- c.   If the manuscript is accepted, you'll be offered a writing contract
- d.   You may be asked to write one book or several books (contract varies)
- e.   You'll be paid an advance; and then royalties if the book does well
- f.   Royalties are based on the cover price of the book (5-10%) typically

B.   Advantages of Traditional Publishing
- You're paid an advance and royalties for your book
- Major publishers have larger channels of distribution
- You'll have access to the best editors, cover designers, etc.

C.   Disadvantages of Traditional Publishing
- You don't have control over pricing or designing your book
- Books will only be on the shelves for three or four months
- Major publishers spend more time promoting top authors

Now that you know the difference between independent, self-publishing, and traditional publishing, you have to decide what you want to do. Some authors spend years trying to find an agent or a publisher, and a few will eventually succeed. Some writers claim that persistence is the key, and it takes time to find a good agent.

Some authors will self-publish while they continue seeking a writing contract. According to a couple of the literary agents that I spoke with, this is the best course to follow. These particular agents surmised that the major publishers are looking for books that have proven sales records. So if you're not a celebrity with a sordid past, like Bill Clinton, they're not willing to take a chance on you as an unknown author. This may be one of the reasons why there is such an increase in self-published authors.

I plan to try an independent publisher.   _____

I want to self-publish my own book.   _____

I plan to pursue a traditional publisher.   _____

I want to try all three ways of publishing.   _____

I'm still undecided.   _____

Barbara Joe-Williams

STEP SIX

SELF-PUBLISHING YOUR BOOK

I can do all things through Christ who strengthens me.

Philippians 4:13

Now that you've made the commitment to self-publishing, it's time to set-up your business office. Yes, writing might be your passion, but publishing is definitely a business venture whether it's full-time or part-time. So let's get it started.

I.   LICENSES

Once you decide to self-publish, you've made a decision to be in business for yourself. Therefore, you must set yourself up as a sole proprietorship business by applying for the proper city and county licenses. In Florida, these licenses must be renewed in September of each year for you to remain a legal business. If you're thinking about publishing other authors at some point, I recommend that you apply to become a Limited Liability Company (LLC) instead of a sole proprietorship.

II.   NAME REGISTRATION

You also have to decide on a business name and register it with your state's Department of Fictitious Name Registration. If you choose to use your own name as the business name, you don't need to pay for this. Each fictitious name registration must be renewed every five years.

I chose the name Amani Publishing because I hope to one day leave my company to my daughter, Amani. Hopefully, she will love reading and publishing as much as I do.

III. EQUIPMENT AND SOFTWARE

Now that you're set-up as an official business, you must designate office space in your home or an outside facility equipped with state-of-the art computer hardware and software along with a printer, facsimile machine, business telephone, and scanner.

Make sure that the computer you purchase has ample memory to accommodate your publishing files. If you're doing your own graphics for the cover, they will take up a lot more memory than text files.

Specific programs that I use:

- Adobe Reader
- Adobe Acrobat 6.0 Standard (PDF)
- Microsoft Word
- Adobe Photoshop 7.0.1
- Microsoft Works Database
- Microsoft Spreadsheets
- Microsoft Picture It! Photo 7.0

I didn't have any idea regarding the significance of a portable document format (PDF) file until I was ready to go to print. The printer informed me that both my cover and text files would have to be converted into PDF files before downloading to their site. I had to go to the Internet to research this new terminology and call a computer programmer to get a clear understanding of what needed to be done.

A PDF file is a convenient and popular method for distributing information electronically. A PDF program will save your document and fonts exactly the way it was created on your computer, and provide security when transporting documents over the web. Once a file is converted to PDF, it cannot be altered in anyway. You also have the option of using a password to restrict access to your files.

However, once the file is converted to PDF, you must make sure that the fonts are properly embedded or it may cause a problem with the printer. (See your instruction manual or contact your printer for more information regarding this).

IV.   OFFICE SUPPLIES

You will need a number of office supplies to set up your new business room. I suggest that you join the Sam's Club and purchase a business credit card. Sam's offer a variety of business supplies in bulk at a reasonable price. In addition, you will receive the advantage of shopping during the early morning hours before the regular club members are admitted inside the store.

This is a sample list of the office supplies that I purchased at Sam's just to get started:

- A box of white copying paper
- A box of #10 white envelopes
- 4 boxes of bubble mailers, size 8 ½" x 11"
- A case of CD-RW discs
- One package of two-part Sales Order Forms (carbonless)
- Two boxes of pens
- A desk lamp
- A three-hole puncher
- A case of 1" notebooks
- One digital camera
- A box of paperclips
- A medium-sized stapler w/staples
- A staple remover
- A case of white-out
- A box of manila folders
- A package of expandable folders

V. P. O. BOX

You might as well go ahead and get a post office box now so that your business mail will not be coming to your home address. And once your book takes off, you don't want uninvited guests showing up at your home asking questions about how you did it.

Even though there are other businesses that offer mail boxes, I chose the United States Postal Service. For one thing, a postal box there costs a lot less than a box of the same size somewhere else. Plus, some of those other mail box services have been known to go out of business overnight, and you would lose a great deal of money if you've paid in advance, or if potential customers are searching for your product at an unknown address.

I purchased a medium sized post office box in order to accommodate large envelopes. This was convenient for me because once the book orders started coming in, I made a lot of trips to the post office anyway. I just made it a point to check my mail box while I was there.

VI. BUSINESS BANK ACCOUNT

I set up a separate bank account under my business name. I like keeping my business funds separate from my personal funds so that I won't be tempted to spend all the profits from my book sales. I chose to use a credit union because it was easier for me to set up a business account with them with fewer restrictions. Some of the major banks have strict requirements for maintaining a business account, like a minimum balance of $1,000.

Having a business account makes it much easier to keep track of your business-related purchases and expenses. I write checks or charge all purchases to my business credit card, and then use my business checking account to pay the invoice at the end of each month. Using this method, I have all of my expenses and payments clearly documented.

VII. ISBN

The International Standard Book Number (ISBN) is a ten-digit number (which has been converted to a thirteen-digit number as of January 2007) that uniquely identifies your product. It must be printed on the back cover of your book in the lower right hand corner.

The ISBN is easily translated into a worldwide compatible barcode format containing the retail price of your book. When it's scanned at the cash register, the price should automatically pop-up on the screen. However, this doesn't mean that the bookstores have to charge the full retail price for your book.

Using their computers, they can transfer the barcode into a sale price that will register in their system. Check with your printer because some of them will charge an additional fee for setting up the barcode on your book while others have it built into the price for printing.

You may purchase ISBNs from R. R. Bowker, the U.S. agency licensed to sell them. They cost nearly $300.00 for a minimum of ten numbers including the bar code service, processing fee, and the registration fee. A print-out form is available from their website, or you may contact them at the following address:

R. R. Bowker
630 Central Avenue
New Providence, NJ 07974
(877) 310-7333
ISBN.org
Isbn-san@bowker.com

It normally takes ten full business days from the date of receipt to process a request for ISBN numbers. If you would like to ask the agency for a faster turn around time, a priority fee of $75 will be included in your bill. Priority service ensures that your request will be processed within 48-hours of receipt.

After you have assigned an ISBN to your book, you should register the information with Books In Print, the industry's largest web-based bibliographic resource for professionals. They can provide stock availability information from more than twenty-five vendors for active and hard to find titles. Their database also includes Print-on-Demand titles distribution. You must be assigned a user name and password for accessing the system. Once you have completed the registration form, it may take up to three business days to activate your password at: **Booksinprint.com**

From then on, you simply log-in for viewing, adding and updating your titles or publisher's information. Sometimes it can take longer than three business days for updates, so please be patient and keep checking for the latest information. If you have questions or concerns, they usually respond quickly to e-mail.

The BowkerLink system provides publishers with an automated tool to keep updating or adding new titles to the Books in Print database. It is a free, easy to use on-line access system that makes your publishing information available to all publishers, distributors, bookstores, and libraries at: **Bowkerlink.com**

VIII. LCCN

You must have a Library of Congress Control Number (LCCN) if you intend for your books to be purchased by libraries. This unique identification number must be printed inside your book on the copyright page.

The library adds the number to their database so that your book will be accessible for ordering from all public library facilities. A card number can even be assigned before your book is published. All you have to do is apply for a Pre-Assigned Catalog Number (PCN) at your convenience.

It doesn't cost anything, and the application can be completed on-line. However, all registered publishers are obligated to send a complimentary copy of their new book immediately upon publication to the Library of Congress at the following address:

> **Library of Congress**
> Cataloging in Publication Division
> 101 Independence Ave., S. E.
> Washington, D. C. 20540-4320
> (202) 707-6372
> **Pcn.loc.gov**

Your continued participation in the PCN program is contingent upon full compliance with this request. The PCN program is separate from the copyright registration.

You will be assigned an account number and a password from the website. It usually takes one to two weeks to process your request to participate in the PCN program.

IX.   ACCOUNTING AND BOOKKEEPING

The accounting and bookkeeping system that you decide to use is strictly up to you. There are all types of office software available for maintaining business records.

I don't use accounting books. I save every expenditure receipt that I get. I keep all of them in a folder in chronological order, and then at the end of the year, I transfer everything into a spreadsheet broken down into the following categories:

- Office expenses
- Mailing expenses
- Traveling and gas
- Printing expenses
- Marketing materials
- Miscellaneous expenses
- Business memberships

I take a printed copy of the spreadsheet to my accountant so that he can figure out the rest. I would never try to do my own business taxes. If you want to calculate whether or not you've made a profit at the end of the year, use the formula below:

Total Expenses – Net sales = Profit/Loss

If you have spent $6,000 on business production and your sales are $4,000 then you have a business loss of $2,000. But if you have spent $6,000 on business and your sales are $8,000 then you have a business profit of $2,000. The breakeven point is when total expenses are equal to net sales.

As far as bookkeeping, I simply use the two-part carbonless Sales Order Form. If I'm invoicing a retail bookstore, I make a note on the Sales Order Form for the total amount that is due. When the payment is received, I record the date that it was paid in full on my copy of the form and make the deposit into my business account.

X.   PAYING TAXES

I know that this is the part that every self-employed person dreads. But you must collect county taxes on every book sold in-state and then report those taxes to the federal government at the end of each quarter. This is a tedious process that requires your undivided attention. Paperwork must be submitted on time or you will be charged with penalties.

I'm not going to try and explain everything about the tax-paying process, but I will clue you in on a few things that you need to be aware of. The first thing that you should do is consult with your local tax office regarding specific requirements for your county and state tax rate.

I attended a Tax Preparation Workshop in my county before going into business. This really helped me with preparing my forms every quarter and understanding the tax laws.

However, I still have to call them on occasion when I have pertinent questions or if there's something that I don't understand. The good news is that you don't have to pay taxes when you purchase your books from the printer. And you don't have to charge taxes when you sell your books to the retail stores or the book distributors because they are tax exempt. They will collect the proper state taxes when they sell the books to their customers. Make a note of this:

You will also have to pay taxes on any books that you give away as promotional copies. The only difference is that you pay taxes on the price that you paid to have the books printed instead of the retail price. Keep a separate list of those "give-away" books for business deductions at the end of the year.

The following checklist is a sample for you to follow when you're ready to start your publishing business. Every set-up is different but it lists the basic things that you should need to get started.

Checklist for Starting a Publishing Business (Sample)

_____ City license

_____ County license

_____ State name registration

_____ Equipment & software

_____ Office supplies

_____ P. O. Box number

_____ Set-up business bank account

_____ ISBN application

_____ Library of Congress application

_____ Hire an accountant

_____ Set up accounting/bookkeeping system

_____ Contact local tax office

_____ Attend a tax seminar

_____ Apply for a business credit card

_____ Order business cards

Barbara Joe-Williams

STEP SEVEN

FORMATTING YOUR BOOK

Along with enthusiasm, dedication and persistence, you've got to be realistic.

Arthur Ashe

This is definitely a critical stage in becoming a successful self-published author. You will be required to make realistic decisions affecting the overall outcome of your printed book. Remember, don't get overwhelmed with this step, simply make one decision at a time and try not to keep second guessing yourself. If you don't have a technical background in computers, you may have to hire a consultant at this stage to cover various parts of your project. Being a self-publisher doesn't mean that you have to do everything yourself. It is okay to contract with other professionals on an as-needed-basis. Just remember that you have the final say.

If you're not sure exactly how you want your finished product to look, then I suggest that you take some time to go visit your local bookstore. Look around in the section of books that are similar to the type of book that you plan to publish. Even though I have over one thousand books in my garage, I still went for a stroll through several of the local bookstores to get fresh ideas. Pay careful attention to the front cover layout, the size of the books, the binding, the fonts, and the back cover layout. Think about how you want your book to be compared to those that you see on the shelf.

Then, mentally visualize your cover stacked beside the others on display. I strongly believe in visualization when it comes to success. You have to be able to see yourself as successful before anyone else can see you that way.

I.   SIZE OF BOOK & BINDING

First, you should determine the size that you want your finished book to be, and whether you want it to be a hardback or a paperback copy. Hardback books are really nice, but they are a lot more expensive to print. You will have to price your book much higher than you would a paperback in order to receive a profitable return on your investment. Most first time independent authors are virtually unknown. Therefore, you would be taking a tremendous risk by printing hardback books without having an established audience interested in purchasing them.

However, if this is your goal, you should take your time researching a printer that can provide you with the best quality hardback. I know a couple of self-publishers that have had their hardbacks printed overseas because they have gotten a much better price on printing over there. While I don't have any contact information on those printers, it would be another alternative for reducing the cost of producing your hardback book. Just be aware that the overseas shipping time will make it take a lot longer to receive your book.

The following sizes are standard for a trade paperback publication: 5" x 8", 5.5" x 8.5", or 6" x 9". If you want a different size, you will have to consult with your printer regarding special sizing costs, which will probably be much higher.

II.   SETTING MARGINS

Once you determine the size of your book, you need to set the margins so that the text will fall evenly between them for a perfect bound copy. Most paperback books are perfect bound because it is the least expensive form of bookbinding. Using this method, some form of adhesive is used to bind the book on the left-hand side so the left margin has to be wider in order to center the text on the page.

At this point, you should also decide whether or not you'd like to have your text justified with the right margin.

For a 6"x 9" book, use the following margins:

1. Top at 1.85"
2. Bottom at 1.65"
3. Left at 1.75"
4. Right at 1.75"
5. Gutter at 0.5"
6. Footer at 1.5"

For a 5.5"x 8.5" book, use the following margins:

1. Top at 2.1"
2. Bottom at 1.9"
3. Left at 2.0"
4. Right at 2.0"
5. Gutter at 0.5"
6. Footer at 1.75"

For a 5"x 8" book, use the following margins:

1. Top at 2.35"
2. Bottom at 2.15"
3. Left at 2.25"
4. Right at 2.25"
5. Gutter at 0.5"
6. Footer at 2.0"

Make sure that you have the pages set to "mirror margins." Then set the spacing for single space so that the computer screen will reflect the exact size and format of your book.

If you're using Microsoft Word, follow these steps for setting the above margins:

1. Click on **File**
2. Click on **Page Setup**
3. Click **Margins**
4. Type in numbers suggested
5. Then click on **OK**

To set footer margins, go back to the **Page Setup** menu, click on **Layout**, type in the footer margin, and then click on **OK.** For more details, refer to the help menu. Now go to the **Insert** menu, click on **Page Numbers** and set up the position and alignment for them.

III. CHOOSING FONTS

Now you're ready to choose a font for your text. I chose to use the popular Times New Roman font in a size twelve for my first book. I wanted a sizeable font so that my novel would be easy reading. I tested out several of them before finally choosing the Times font. These are some other popular fonts that you might want to consider: Arial, Baskerville Old Face, Book Antiqua, Bookman Old Style, Century Gothic, Courier, Garamond, Helvetica, Optima, and Palatino.

Of course, the larger the font, the more pages you'll have. Once you've set your margins and chosen a font size, it won't be necessary to guess at how many pages your finished manuscript will be, you can keep track of them as you write. If you're aiming for a certain number of published pages, then you should keep adjusting the font size until you have exactly what you want.

Most printers suggest that you keep the font size between nine and thirteen points for text. They also suggest that you use between fourteen and eighteen points for the title and subtitles. For the text of this book, I'm also using a Times New Roman twelve point font.

IV.   CHOOSING THE FRONT COVER

While you're working on your manuscript, you should be thinking of ideas for the front cover of your book. I had finished my first manuscript, and I was still at a loss for a cover. Fortunately, I was on vacation visiting a relative when I fell in love with the picture I eventually used for the front cover of, *Forgive Us This Day*. When I first laid eyes on this photograph, I knew it would be the perfect cover for my romance novel. After contacting the photographer and securing a copyright release to use the picture, I was ready to design my front cover. So, I took the photo to FedEx Kinko's Copy Center, told them what I wanted, and the next day I had a PDF cover file. It took several tries before they got it exactly the way I'd imagined it to be, but it was worth the effort.

Some publishers spend hundreds of dollars on designing and formatting their front covers. The total cost of my cover file was less than $100.00, including the price of the photograph and the copyright release. I was really blessed to find that photograph when I did because I had been searching websites for a picture to use on my front cover. Most of them wanted anywhere from $100 to $1,000 for just one photograph.

Since then, I've found two fabulous websites where you can download photographs for $1 to $15 each (depending on the size of the picture). Membership is free, and you can download as many as you like each month. They have a vast collection of beautiful royalty-free pictures taken by amateur photographers who are seeking exposure for their work. Royalty-free means that you pay a one time fee to download photographs to be used however you please.

Check them out at the following websites for royalty-free photographs:

A.   **IStockPhoto.com**
     1202-20 Avenue SE
     Calgary AB Y26 1MB
     Canada
     (403) 265-3062
     (403) 262-2582
     (866) 478-6251

B.   **BigStockPhoto.com**
     2919 Bellows Ct.
     Davis, CA 95616
     (530) 852-4867

V.   DETERMINING THE SPINE

The spine of the book connects the front cover to the back cover and usually contains the book title, author, and publisher's logo. In order to determine the spine width, you have to know the final page count and the weight of the paper that you'll be using to print your books. However, spine size can be calculated by dividing the number of pages by the pages per inch (PPI) of the paper used. So if you have a 200 page book and the PPI is 200, then your spine size will be one-inch thick. You must have at least eighty pages of text in order to have the title printed on the spine of your book.

You will have to get the exact PPI from your printer because they all use different paper. The standard paper weight for soft back books is 50# white offset with a 512 PPI or 55# crème with 444 PPI. Most paperback covers are printed on white, 80# cover stock, and laminated for a glossy finish.

For example, my 272 page novel had a 512 PPI and my spine was set at .53: 272/512 = .53

Some publishers like to design their own logo to be placed on their books. Initially, I choose a simple format for my Amani Publishing logo using keys on the keyboard: **[AP].**

If you want to create a more elaborate symbol for your company's image, then go ahead and be creative or pay someone to design it for you. If you'd like to register your symbol as a trademark, contact the United States Patent and Trademark Office by calling (800) 786-9199 or visit their website at: **uspto.gov**

VI.   PREPARING THE BACK COVER

The back cover serves as a synopsis for your book, and it should be written long before you've completed your manuscript. This is how you're really going to sell books. You may grab readers' attention with the front cover, but the back of the book is what motivates a true reader to buy or not buy your product.

You don't want to give away all of the details so try not to make the synopsis too long. Just give the readers enough to make them want to read more.

Don't waste space on the back cover repeating the title of your book. Get right to the meat of your storyline. I chose to use questions on my first back cover because I wanted to give the reader something to think about right away.

Be sure to include a short biography about yourself or a short statement. Some authors like to have their picture on the back cover, but I chose not to do that. You must also make sure that you have the book price and the ISBN on the back cover. Some distributors will not accept your book if the price is not printed on the backside.

The front cover, spine, and back cover have to be created as a single page layout. Check with your printer before converting the file to a PDF because you may have to add a little more space for the final trimming of the book. This is called a "bleed," which is usually .125" added to the cover size.

VII.   PRICING YOUR BOOK

Determining the price of a book is always a dilemma for the self-published author. The average price for independently published books ranges from $9.95 to $19.95 depending on the genre and the number of pages contained in the manuscript.

The bottom line on pricing is how many books you can sell and what your profit margin will be. Your profit from each book will be based on where the books are sold. If you're selling on your own or from your website, you'll receive all of the profits for yourself. However, if you're selling directly to a bookstore, the standard discount for them is 40% which means that you will receive 60% of the cover price. Now once you sign on with a distributor, they will take an additional 15% of the cover price. So in essence, you'll receive 45% of the retail cost. Plus, you're responsible for paying the freight charges. With this in mind, you want to try and sell as many books as you can on your own through non-store book signings, conferences, workshops, or other creative outlets.

The real profit is the difference between the cover price and the printing cost. If the retail price is $13.95 and the printing cost per book was $3.95, then you've made a $10 profit on every book that you sell directly to a customer. As I've said before, once you start dealing with bookstores and distributors, that profit margin will change significantly.

XIII.   INTERIOR PAGES

Once you have completed the manuscript, determined the binding, and selected a cover for your book, it's time to put the interior pages in order. There are extra pages that must be included in the front and back of your book.

A.   Title Page

The title page is usually the first page of a book. It normally includes the title, subtitle (if used), author's name, publisher's name, company slogan or logo, and trademark if available.

B.   Copyright page

The second page is normally the copyright page, and it must include the © symbol followed by the year even if you're not filing with the official copyright office. To make this sign using Microsoft Word, simply pull down the **Insert** menu, click on **symbol**, and then double click on the circled c.

In addition, if you're writing a fictional novel, this is the disclaimer page for characters, names, and places. You may include the publisher's name and mailing address along with the e-mail and website addresses.

If you have an ISBN and/or a Library of Congress Number, it must be shown on the copyright page. You should use this page to credit the photographer, cover designers, illustrators, writers, or other contributors. It may also include a reference to the printing date, number of copies printed, and the printer's name and location.

C.   Other Pages

There are a few other pages that you may wish to include such as the table of contents, foreword, introduction, bibliography, acknowledgements, appendages, references, dedication, glossary, book reviews, illustrations, or an index. You may also wish to include an order form at the end of the book for taking future orders. And you may want to leave several blank pages at the end for readers to make notes.

IX.   FINAL NUMBER OF MANUSCRIPT PAGES

Once you've decided on the format (or layout) of your book, you need to determine your final page count. This will be very important for when you start contacting printers regarding your book.

The rule of thumb is that you must have an even number of pages, but some printers require that the number be divisible by 2, 4, or 16, depending on the type of printing press that's being used.

For instance, if the requirement is that your number of pages be divisible by 16, you would have to format according to the following scale even if you have to add blank pages to get the proper count:

16
32
48
64
80
96
112
128
144
160
176
192
208
224
240
256
272
288
304
320
336
352
368
384
400, etc.

Barbara Joe-Williams

Take a few minutes to make some notes on how your book will be formatted.

1. My final page count is   _____

2. My book size will be   _____

3. My cover will be   _____

4. My top book margin is   _____

5. My bottom book margin is   _____

6. My left book margin is   _____

7. My right book margin is   _____

8. I will use this type of font   _____

9. I will use this size font   _____

10. My book spine is   _____

11. The price of my book is   _____

12. I want to include other pages _____

13. If yes, list them here _____

_____

_____

Barbara Joe-Williams

STEP EIGHT

PRINTING YOUR BOOK

I used to want the words "She tried" on my tombstone. Now I want the words "She did it."

Katherine Dunham

Pat yourself on the back. You've completed the first seven steps! Now it's time to start searching for a printer. Actually, this is a step that you could be working on in conjunction with the other steps. It would be great to contact printers early in the game and allow enough time for them to send you sample books before you're ready to print your project.

You should take your time selecting a printer. Choose someone that will give you quality along with a reasonable price. Sometimes the cheapest price is not always the best price, especially in the publishing industry. I learned this lesson the hard way when I decided to go with a cheaper printer to keep my production costs low. Well, I ended up spending more money because I had to send the entire order back. Plus, I paid the shipping and handling costs. And even though the sample book looked decent; the final order did not meet my satisfaction. Therefore, I filed a dispute claim with my credit card company and was reimbursed for the printing costs.

Make sure that you place your book order in time to allow for printing and shipping delays. I've seen authors show up for book signings without any books because their shipment didn't arrive in time. You don't want that to happen to you. So plan ahead, and make sure that you have your book order in your hands before scheduling personal appearances.

I.   SPECIFICATIONS

Now, how do you know the specifications for your book? Well, I contacted a local printer and made an appointment with one of their sales representatives. She showed me samples of cover stock, various paper colors and weights, along with sample books. She also gave me a copy of the completed specification form to take with me for future reference.

Once I learned the details regarding specifications, I was able to search the Internet and complete these forms on-line for various printers. If you're not sure about the quantity right now, you may enter various figures to see what will be more economical for your business. For instance, you may request a quote based on 100, 200, 300, 400, and 800 copies.

A specification form will usually require that you give some of the following information regarding your book:

- Book title
- Book size
- Paperback
- Hardback
- Number of text pages
- Graphics needed
- Color of text
- Paper color
- Paper weight
- Cover weight
- 1 or 2-color cover
- Full-color cover
- Matte cover
- Laminated cover
- Perfect binding
- Saddle stitch binding
- Quantity needed

II.   TYPES OF PRINTERS

Let's take a look at the different types of printers that are available to self-published authors.

A.   Traditional Printers

Most traditional printing houses don't like to run less than 1,000 copies at a time. Their best deals will be on print runs of 1,000 to 10,000 copies. If you're confident that you can sell this many copies on a first run, then this will probably be the route for you to go. However, there are other options.

Here's the traditional printer that I visited for specifications:

Rose Printing Company, Inc.
2503 Jackson Bluff Road
Tallahassee, FL 32304
(850) 576-4151
Roseprinting.com

B.   Short Run Printers

If you're interested in printing less than a thousand books, you should consider a Short-Run Printer. They normally specialize in printing anywhere from 100 to 2,000 copies at a time.

For my first book printing, I used King Printing in Lowell, Massachusetts. But after my initial run, they went up on their prices tremendously. I'm not endorsing any printer, but here's a sample list of some short-run printers that you might want to contact for more information:

1.   Adibooks
181 Industrial Avenue
Lowell, MS 01852
(978) 458-2345
(978) 458-3026
Adibooks.com

2.   **Alumni Graphics**
       1560 Newbury Road #230
       Newbury Park, CA 91320
       (877) 336-7244
       (805) 499-4319
       Alumnigraphics.com

3.   **BookMasters**
       2541 Ashland Road
       Mansfield, OH 44905
       (800) 537-6727
       (429) 589-4040
       Bookmasters.com

4.   **BooksjustBooks**
       51 East 42nd Street
       New York, NY 10017
       (800) 621-2556
       (212) 681-8002
       Booksjustbooks.com

5.   **Central Plains Book Manufacturing**
       22234 C Street
       Strother Field
       Winfield, KS 67156
       (877) 278-2726
       (620) 221-4762
       Centralplainsbook.com

6.   **Color House Graphics**
       3505 Eastern Avenue
       Grand Rapids, MI 49508
       (800) 454-1916
       (616) 245-5494
       Colorhousegraphics.com

7.   **Publishers Graphics**
     140 Della Court
     Carol Stream IL 60188
     (888) 404-3769
     (630) 221-1870
     Pubgraphics.com

8.   **Sheridan Books**
     613 East Industrial Drive
     Chelsea, MI 48118
     (734) 475-9145
     (734) 475-7337
     Sheridanbooks.com

9.   **SPS Publications**
     800 South Avenue
     Eustis, FL 32726
     (352) 357-2665
     (352) 357-7166
     Spspublication.com

10. **Whitehall Printing Company**
     4244 Corporate Square
     Naples, FL 34104-4753
     (800) 321-9290
     (239) 643-6429
     Whitehallprinting.com

Check with your printer regarding the cost of reprints after the initial run is depleted. Some printers will charge a little less while others will go up on the price or remain the same. You need to be aware of this ahead of time in case you decide to change printers.

There is one website that you can visit, put in all the specifications for your book, and then individual printers from across the globe will automatically contact you offering their bids. That website is located at: **Printindustry.com**

C.   Print-On-Demand Printers

Another option, called Print-On-Demand (POD) printing, is gaining in popularity as an alternative way to self-publish. Using this method, your completed manuscript and cover files are e-mailed to the POD printer, and they will print them according to your specifications.

With print on demand technology, books are printed up as they are needed. You can order one book to be printed or 1,000 at any time at the same cost per book. So you're not responsible for warehousing a large inventory. Books can be ordered directly from the POD printer and shipped from their location as orders are received. This will take some of the burden off of your shoulders and give you more free time to concentrate on your other writing projects.

However, one disadvantage with POD printing is that you normally have to pay a slightly higher price for each book printed than you would pay with a traditional printer. But the turn-around time is faster, and the quality is usually even better.

After careful consideration, I decided to try Lightning Source, Inc. for the printing of my third and subsequent books. They are a subsidiary of Ingram Book Distributors providing printing and book distribution services. So far, I've been pleased with their services.

Here's their contact information:

1.   **Lightning Source, Inc.**
     1246 Heil Quaker Blvd.
     La Vergne, TN 37086
     (615) 231-5815
     Lightningsource.com

Here's another POD printer that was recommended to me:

2.   **Axess Printing**
       P. O. Box 500835
       Atlanta, GA 31150
       (770) 888-3082
       Axessprinting.com

III.   DECIDING HOW MANY BOOKS TO PRINT

The next major decision you will have to make is deciding how many books to print for the initial run. Most authors like to start with one thousand books because you get a better price when you order larger quantities (if you're using a traditional printer). For instance, if you order one thousand books you may pay only $3 per book, whereas if you order 500 books at one time, you may pay $5 per book. Volume is the key if you can afford it.

Of course, the decision you make at this point will depend on the budget that you have left. I chose not to print one thousand copies because my budget would only allow for me to print 400 copies of my first novel. Besides, as a beginning author without any prior writing experience or a distributor, I was leery of ordering one thousand books to start. Based on my years of reading, I know that it's extremely hard for dedicated readers to take a chance on a new author. If you like to read, you have favorite writers that you enjoy, and it's difficult to take a chance on a new writer because you may not like their writing style.

The best thing about dealing with a short-run or POD printer is that you don't have to buy a lot of copies. You can order a few books just to test the market. Give yourself a timeline for selling those, and then order more the next time. It was my goal to sell 400 books in four months, then take that money and recycle it back into my business. My strategy worked.

So far, I have been able to maintain my goal of selling at least 100 books a month. It has taken consistent marketing and promotions to accomplish this task. However, if you believe that you can sell 1,000 or 5,000 copies your first time out and you can afford the payment, then go for it! You'll make more money in the long run. The bottom line is that you should print the amount of books that you believe you can easily sell.

I have also found the following advantages to ordering fewer copies:

A.   They don't require as much storage space.

B.   You're not stuck with a lot of extra copies, if the books don't sell within your time limit.

C.   If you don't like the final printed version, you won't have a lot of copies to return.

D.   You don't have a huge sum of money tied up into inventory.

E.   If you find any errors on the short run, they can be corrected before placing a large order.

If you're on a budget or your money is running low, order a small number of books that you can sell on your own at a full profit. Then, take that money and keep ordering additional books until you can make your way to ordering larger quantities of at least one thousand at a time.

At any rate, you should be prepared to give away at least 10% of your shipment as promotional copies to the media, bookstores, and the book distributors. They will be considered promotional expenses just like flyers and postcards so they will be tax deductible, too.

IV.   SELECTING A PRINTER

Now that you have determined your book specifications, have various printer bids, and know how many copies you want for the first run, it's time to select a printer. The best advice that I can give you at this point is to go with your gut feelings from the printers that you have been corresponding with.

If possible, check with other self-published authors for printer recommendations before making a final selection. Take a look at the quality of their books and ask questions. This is the step where you don't want to be disappointed, so proceed with caution.

Be sure to pay special attention to the printer's contract regarding their overrun policy. Some short-run printers won't guarantee an exact number of copies because they usually have a 5 to 10% overrun. In this case, some printers expect you to purchase the extra copies while others will give you the option of whether or not to buy them now or later. Of course, using a POD printer eliminates this step.

A.   Downloading Files

As soon as you select a printer, you will be required to download your files to their website. Depending on the size of your files, you may be able to send them as an e-mail attachment like I did. Either way, the material will have to be converted into a PDF file.

As I mentioned earlier, I didn't have any understanding of a PDF file until after I had selected a printer and was about to send my documents. My lack of knowledge in this subject caused me to have almost a week's delay in getting my files to the printer. I had to pay a computer expert to convert the files for me.

Now I have the software loaded on my own computer, and I can have the files converted in a matter of minutes. Please note that a PDF file can't be changed once the conversion process is completed.

B. Proofs

Once your files are downloaded to the printer's production site, it will take the company approximately 3 to 5 working days to provide you with a proof. The first proof is usually provided free of charge. If you want to make any additional changes after that point, you will be billed accordingly.

On the printing of my first novel, *Forgive Us This Day*, it took three proofs before I was satisfied with the final text. The errors were entirely my fault. There were little things that I kept seeing that I thought had been changed in my rush to get it to the printer. Don't make that mistake; it can be costly.

After you have approved the final proof, there is a huge discrepancy between printers in the turnaround time. Some printers guarantee that they will have your printing complete in 5 to 10 working days while others may take from 10 to 15 working days. Yet, others may claim that it will take at least 6 to 8 weeks. Your decision will depend on a variety of factors including the cost of printing and your immediate needs. For instance, one printer may have a low price, but it may take the business up to eight weeks to print your books. If you're willing to wait, then that's fine. On the other hand, one printer may have a slightly higher price, but the company can guarantee that your order will be completed within 10 to 15 working days. It's your final call.

C. Delivery Date

Try to confirm a delivery date with your printer as soon as the books are ready. Allow enough time for whichever shipping method you both have agreed to use.

Make sure that you receive the tracking numbers for your books as soon as they are shipped. This way, you know exactly what day to expect your order. If you're using Federal Express or United Parcel Service, you can monitor your packages from their websites. Simply type in the tracking numbers and it will show you where your package is located at any given date.

When your packages are delivered to your home, unpack them to make sure that you have the correct number of books. Once, I ordered 100 books from a printer, but when I counted them out, I only had 90 books. I sent the entire shipment back to him the next day. So be sure that you account for your books upon receipt.

Check your packing list or invoice to make sure that the charges to your account are correct. Call the printer immediately if any discrepancies are noted. If necessary, notify your credit card company regarding any unresolved issues. That's the good thing about using a credit card for your business purchases. If there's a problem with a shipment, your cash is not tied up for months, and you don't have to take legal actions to be reimbursed. The credit card company will handle that for you once you file a dispute claim with them.

V. E-BOOKS

Once you've decided which printer to use for the hardcopy of your book, you should also consider converting your manuscript into an e-Book. An e-Book is simply an electronic file of your book and they normally sell for a fraction of the cost of a hardback or paperback copy because the customer is only paying to download the file. They'll be able to read the book from their computer screen or print it out on their own paper to read at their leisure.

The average price to download an e-Book ranges from $2.00 to $10.00. However, you're only paying the cost to convert the manuscript into a PDF and the payment processing fee if it's transmitted via the Internet. So you're definitely making more of a profit this way. The only problem is that a lot of people have not caught on to e-Books or downloading books yet.

I conducted a survey on e-Books after publishing my first novel. The majority of my customers preferred hard books to e-Books but many said that they would consider the possibility or would appreciate having the option.

VI.   AUDIO BOOKS

Another alternative to printing a hardcopy book is to have your book read onto a cassette tape or compact disc. I've heard some people say that this is the most convenient way for them to experience a book because they're constantly on the go and they can listen to the book while they're in the car running their daily errands or on the way to and from work. Either way you look at it, it's an opportunity to reach more people with your work.

I'm ready to print my manuscript.   _____

I've decided on a printer.   _____

I've decided on the number to print.   _____

I need more time to think about this process.   _____

I'm interested in doing an e-Book.   _____

I'd like to have my books on audio.   _____

STEP NINE

DISTRIBUTING YOUR BOOK

Success is measured not so much by the position that one has reached in life as by the obstacles which he has overcome while trying to succeed.

Booker T. Washington

You're almost there! One more major step after this one and you'll be on the way to pursuing your dreams with new meaning and determination. Now that you have your new books in hand, let me introduce you to the world of distribution.

A distributor is the middle man, and is responsible for getting books into the bookstores nationwide as well as on-line. This is important because most major bookstores like Barnes & Noble will not carry your book unless you have a distributor. They don't like dealing with independent publishers because they would have to monitor too many accounts since self-publishing is on the rise.

Here's a simplified formula:

Bookstore—Distributor—Printer (POD) or Publisher

Distribution can be both a nightmare and a dream come true for self-published authors. Distributors take a big chunk of your profits on one hand. But on the other hand, they can get your books into nationwide bookstores (which generally leads to more recognition for a new author). While your profits are less, you are steadily selling more books. I try to put this into perspective by thinking that if I can make just $1 a sale and sell a million books, then I'll be a millionaire in the long run. So far, I haven't sold a million copies, but anything is possible in this business.

I.   CHOOSING A DISTRIBUTOR

You can try selling your books on your own, but you will probably sell a lot more copies at a faster rate if you sign on with a distributor. I wasted valuable time trying to get around the distribution process, but several months into the game, I decided to give it a try. However, you should be able to get into your local bookstores without having a distributor. But for nationwide ordering, you need a major player.

I waited about three or four months after my book was published before I really started looking for a distributor. I tried unsuccessfully to get my books into the major retail bookstores on my own. Once I was accepted by a major distributor, the following stores eventually ordered my book:

- Barnes & Noble Booksellers

- Borders Books

- Books-A-Million

Whereas I had been barely selling a hundred books a month, suddenly I was selling well over that amount. While it doesn't cost you any cash money to sign on with a distributor, they typically want a 55% discount with 90-day net payment terms. If you're dealing directly with the bookstore, they expect to receive the standard 40% discount with a 30-day net payment plan. This means that you will have your money in 30 to 90 days depending on your agreement with the distributor. Therefore, you need additional money or credit available to maintain the business while you're waiting on payments which could exceed your initial investment.

Each distributor has specific submission guidelines that you will have to follow if you want to increase your chances of becoming accepted by them. Usually, they will ask for you to write a personal letter describing yourself and your product in detail.

Barbara Joe-Williams

They also want to know what steps you have taken to market your book before considering your application. Here's a list of the major distributors that I have researched for you on the Internet:

1. A & B Book Distributors

This is a wholesaler specializing in African-American books, tapes, and gifts. They offer contracts based on a quarterly consignment agreement. You may reach them at the following address:

A & B Book Distributors
1000 Atlantic Avenue
Brooklyn, NY 11238
(718) 783-7808

2. African World Book Distributors

They also specialize in distributing African-American books.

African World Book Distributors
2217 Pennsylvania Avenue
Baltimore, MD 21217
(410) 383-2006

3. American Wholesale Book Company

This is the only company that Books-A-Million uses for their distribution. You may contact your local BAM store manager for an application package. Titles submitted to AWBC must have the following: ISBN, EAN barcode, and the price printed on the back cover. No stapled books will be accepted. They also require that you submit two complimentary copies for their review:

American Wholesale Book Company
ATTENTION: New Acquisitions
131 S. 25th Street
Irondale, AL 35210
(205) 956-4151, ext. 300

4. Anderson Merchandisers

This is the only way to get your book into Wal-mart and Sam's Club. They request that you send in a letter of introduction and one copy of your book. Normally, they only stock the books from the best seller's list at Wal-mart, but it's still worth a try.

Anderson Merchandisers
ATTENTION: Marketing Department
New Title Solicitation
814 S. W. Raintree Lane
Bentonville, AR 72712
(800) 999-0904
(479) 273-0293

5. Baker & Taylor Books

They are a full-line distributor of books, videos, and music products to Internet and traditional retailers. They require that you send one copy of your book for review along with any promotional materials that you have developed.

Baker & Taylor Books
ATTENTION: Buying Department
1120 Route 22 East
P. O. Box 6885
Bridgewater, NJ 08807-2944
(908) 541-7459
(908) 541-7862
BTOL.com

6. C & B Books Distribution

C & B Books' main goal is to introduce authors to the public by supporting them with the sale of their book. This is an African-American owned bookstore that will carry your product based on a six-month consignment agreement. It used to be strictly an on-line bookstore, but now it has grown into a retail store.

C & B Books Distribution
P. O. Box 671155
Flushing, NY 11367
(917) 225-3575
(917) 515-0914
(718) 591-4525
CBBooksdistribution.com

7. Christian Book Distributors

They are a distributor of Christian books, media, software, and gifts. They also sell Bibles, church supplies, and clothing.

Christian Book Distributors
(800) 247-4784
(978) 977-5010
Christianbook.com

8. Ingram Book Group

This is the largest book distributor in the United States. It is my understanding that you must have at least ten titles or more in print to be considered by them. This is the only contact information that I have for them:

Ingram Book Group
One Ingram Blvd.
La Vergne, TN 37086-1986
(615) 793-5000
Ingrambook.com

9. Lushena Book Distributors/Publishers

This wholesaler specializes in titles by African-American authors and publishers. You may contact them at the following address:

Lushena Book Distributors
607 Country Club Drive, Unit E
Bensenville, IL 60106
(630) 238-8708
Lushenabks@yahoo.com

10.   Nubian Heritage
This is another wholesale book distributor specializing in African-American books.

Nubian Heritage
2037 5th Avenue
New York, NY 10035
(212) 427-8999

11.   Rittenhouse Book Distributors
They are distributors of healthcare and medical information books.

Rittenhouse Book Distributors, Inc.
511 Feheley Drive
King of Prussia, PA 19406
(800) 345-6425
(800) 223-7488
Rittenhouse.com

12.   Southern Book Service
This is one of the distributors used by Barnes & Noble Bookstores.

Southern Book Services
5154 N. W. 165th Street
Miami Lakes, FL 33014
(800) 766-3254
(305) 621-0425
Southernbook.com

Please note that you will have to adhere to the strict submission guidelines for each distributor which includes sending one or two non-returnable books for their review. Normally, it takes at least six weeks before they will send you a letter stating whether or not your application has been accepted for ordering through their database.

If you receive a letter in two or three weeks, that means that your application has probably been denied. But don't let that discourage you from pressing on. I was turned down by three distributors on this list before Baker & Taylor finally accepted my application. I was about to give up on ever getting a distributor when they e-mailed me with the good news.

II.   CONTACTING BOOKSTORES

Now that you have a major distributor, it's up to you to contact the bookstores requesting that they order your book. Again, you may have to send a detailed letter along with one or two non-returnable copies of your book. This is where you really have to be patient because it will take some time for the bookstores to contact you.

In most cases, you'll have to keep calling them until you have a definite answer. Your persistence will eventually pay off. Again, it may take at least six weeks to hear from the major bookstores. In the meantime, keep pushing your books through other mediums.

A.   Local Bookstores/Church Bookstores

The very first retailers that I contacted were locally owned (independent) bookstores. They were happy to support a local author and most of them gave me a "front of the store" display for several months.

If you've written a Christian book, you should also try to have your work displayed in the local church bookstores. Local and national Christian bookstores, like LifeWay, would definitely be a smart choice.

B.   College Bookstores

The next place that I contacted was my alma mater, Florida A&M University Bookstore, which is owned and operated by Barnes & Noble College Bookstores. The bookstore manager took my information including a copy of my press release and personally sent it to the corporate office.

I didn't know that this facility was a separate entity from their retail store. I thought that once my book was in the college bookstores database that it would be available at all Barnes & Noble store as well, but I was wrong. After months of calling and searching for my title to show up at Barnes & Noble Retail Stores, I was informed that they were two different businesses, and that I needed to send another package of information to the retail main corporate office. Just imagine how disappointed I was!

Well, I didn't let that stop me. I got another package together, put it in the mail, and waited for Barnes & Noble to contact me again. I knew that since my book was already in the database for the college bookstore, that the main bookstore would probably accept it, too. A few weeks later, they did.

You should contact your local college and/or university to see who has ownership of their store. The bookstore manager will provide you with the information for contacting the corporate office.

C. Black-owned Bookstores

It has been my desire to make my book available in many black-owned bookstores. So far, that has proven to be a difficult task. However, I haven't given up on them yet.

There is an on-line directory where you can get a listing of all the nationwide African-American owned bookstores divided by states at:

1. **Authorsontour.com/bookstores.htm**

2. **Mosiacbooks.com**

D.   Amazon.com

Once my book was accepted into the Baker & Taylor database, it was automatically available on-line at the Amazon Bookstore for ordering. I simply had to e-mail them with a request to carry my book. Later, I uploaded the book cover file to my page. However, with many of the POD printers, your cover image is automatically uploaded to this website.

E.   Major Bookstores

Once my book was accepted at Barnes & Noble Retail Stores, Borders, and Books-A-Million Bookstores, it was automatically listed with their on-line bookstores at:

- Barnesandnoble.com

- Booksamillion.com

- Bordersstores.com

Barnes & Noble and Books-A-Million requested one review copy, and Borders asked for two review copies along with an introductory letter and promotional materials also referred to as a press kit. Remember, the American Wholesale Book Company (AWBC) is the only distributor for Books-A-Million Bookstore.

Here are the mailing addresses that I used:

1.   Barnes & Noble Booksellers
Small Press Department
122 5th Avenue
New York, NY 10011
(800) 422-7717

2.   Borders Group, Inc.
New Vendor Acquisitions
100 Phoenix Drive
Ann Arbor, MI 48108
(734) 477-1100

F.   Consignment Bookstores

Some retail stores or gift shops will be amenable to selling your books on consignment for a standard commission. This means that they will stock a number of books in their store and then pay you after the books have sold.

A consignment contract is usually offered for a two to six month time period. If the books sell before the maximum time allowed, you're entitled to full payment.

III.   FILLING ORDERS

Now that you have your printed books, a distributor, and you're in the database for a major bookstore, you're ready to start filling orders. Make sure that you have stored your books in a clean, dry place. Keep them sealed in the original boxes that they were shipped in until you need them. Hopefully, you won't have to worry about keeping them in storage too long.

This is what I did with my first book: I stacked the nine boxes on an eight-foot folding table in my garage. I put one box of books in my van and another box in my home office. Then, I stood there in that garage and imagined one box of books disappearing from that table one at a time until they were all gone. Approximately, four months later, they were.

Visualization is a powerful tool. If you can't visualize yourself as a successful person, then chances are that you will never be one. Start believing in yourself and step out on faith. That's exactly what I did.

You need to have a system in place for filling your orders once they start coming in. The first thing that I do when I receive an order via the Internet, distributor, bookstore or local customer is to write out a receipt and record all the available information at the top of the form.

Then, based on the size of the order, I get the appropriate mailing package. Once the envelope or box is stuffed, sealed, and addressed, I'm off to the post office or other shipping center.

If you're using a POD printer, most of them will handle the orders directly from the distributor, the online bookstores, and retail bookstore for you. So you don't have to worry about shipping to these places.

A.   Mailing Options
You have several options for mailing out your new book. You may want to try each of these before making a final decision.

1.   United States Postal Services (USPS)
If you take your packages to the post office, you should ask for the special media mail rate. This is a lower rate that is available only for shipping books and educational materials. I recommend that you add the extra cents for the delivery confirmation receipt. You can review the complete mailing rate scale at their website located at: **USPS.com**

Media mail can sometimes be very slow (up to 30 days), and there is not a guaranteed delivery date. However, normally deliveries are made in 2 – 14 days. If you prefer to use FedEx or UPS, they will guarantee ground shipment in 1 – 5 days. Their price rate varies based on the final delivery destination.

You will have to decide how much to charge your clients for shipping and handling based upon the delivery method that you choose. I started out using media mail, but I have decided to also use alternative methods for shipping certain packages.

Priority mail is another option available from USPS. This is a little more costly but it's speedier, and you don't have to buy the mailing packages because they're provided by the post office.

2.   FexEx/UPS/DHL

You'll need a credit card to establish an account with one of these services. Once that's in place, you can drop-off packages at the nearest location to you or call to have them picked up (for additional charges) from your place of business.

Another convenience of dealing with them is that most of the work can be completed on-line, and then you simply have to print out a mailing label to paste on the shipping box. They will electronically inform you of the tracking numbers and delivery confirmations.

B.   Following-up on Delivery

For USPS, it is important that you pay the additional cost for the "Delivery Confirmation" if you want to know for sure that your packages have arrived at their destination. For a few cents more, you will know the exact date and time that it was received by your clients, but you will not be able to track the shipping route.

If you use FedEx, UPS, or DHL ground shipping, real tracking will be available from their websites with guaranteed delivery at:

- Fedex.com

- Ups.com

- DHL.com

C.   Direct Shipping from Printer

This is one service that you may need once your book takes off and orders are coming in faster than you can fill them. Once I got below a hundred books from my initial run of 400, I decided it was time to order more books.

Well, suddenly the book took off overnight and I received orders totaling over 200 books before the second run was ready. So I called my printer, ordered more books, and asked him if he could do a direct shipment for me to my distributor's four warehouse locations. Luckily, he was very accommodating.

With that in mind, you might want to make sure that this is one of the services that your selected printer can provide. Of course, you're responsible for paying the shipping either way, so it's up to the printer whether or not he wants to provide this additional service at an extra charge.

I just didn't see any point in him shipping boxes to me that I would have to count and re-box for shipping, take to the post office, and stand in a long line to mail when he could simply print and ship directly. It was certainly much faster and cheaper for me. I simply e-mailed him the mailing labels and the packing lists to be enclosed with each order. It was also a step of faith that paid off in the end. I had to trust that he would handle this properly.

However, using Lightning Source, Inc., I can choose to have book orders from the distributors and bookstores sent directly to them for fulfillment. They will pay LSI the wholesale price of each book and in return, LSI will pay me whatever is left after deducting the cost of printing and shipping.

IV. BOOK RETURNS

Unfortunately, you may be faced with the prospect of handling book returns. When you make your books available to the bookstores through a distributor, they have to be designated "returnable" or the bookstores will not order them. Therefore, even though they may order hundreds of books from you, many of them may be returned after only three or four months on the bookshelves if they haven't sold.

Don't let this process get you down. Just recognize it as a part of the publishing business. Normally, books are returned in good condition which means that you can still make a full profit from them. However, some books maybe returned as "damaged product" which means that you have to find other avenues for handling them.

Here's a list of possible suggestions for returned books:

A. Sell them at a discount price at your personal booking events and book fairs.

B. Offer them at a discount price on-line at **eBay.com** or **Amazon.com**

C. Mail them out to various book clubs and book reviewers as promotional products.

D. Donate some of them to charitable organizations and write them off on your tax returns.

E. Give them away as birthday or holiday gifts.

I have a distribution plan in place.   _____

I will be my own distributor.   _____

I plan to eventually get a distributor.   _____

I have a plan for handling book returns.   _____

Part III

Marketing

Barbara Joe-Williams

STEP TEN

MARKETING YOUR NEW BOOK

For every one of us who succeeds, it's because there's somebody there to show us the way.

Oprah Winfrey

Congratulations! You have made it to the final step. This is another phase that will take some effort, time, and a little money on your part to become successful and maintain quality standards. Now that you've made it this far, it's time to promote your new book and let the world know that you have arrived as an author. Doesn't that sound exciting?

You should be prepared to do some traveling and personal appearances as well as other community projects in order to promote your business. I believe that marketing is the real key to success, and I will share with you how I did it.

I could have the best product in the world, but if people don't know about it, they can't buy it. That's why I made a conscious decision to concentrate on promoting my book the first year. Now that I'm a full-time writer and publisher, every day is filled with calling, writing, or e-mailing someone regarding an update of my book business, scheduling another workshop, contacting another bookstore, or revising my website to keep it updated.

I have used a combination of mediums since the release of my first novel including a website, postcards, press releases, newspapers, radio, television, flyers, book clubs, bookstores, book signings, conferences, festivals, and workshops. Remember, most of your expenses will be tax deductible so just hold on to your receipts.

I.   MARKETING STRATEGIES

Marketing is a major part of publishing your manuscript. Although it's last in this book, it shouldn't be last on your mind.

A.   Low Cost or No Cost Marketing

Believe it or not, marketing doesn't have to be an expensive venture. Let's take a look at my inexpensive marketing strategies.

1.   Using Word of Mouth

This is still the best form of advertising known to mankind. The first thing that you have to do before the book is ever published is start telling everybody that you come in contact with about your future book. Start spreading the word now and you'll reap the rewards a lot sooner.

My family and friends knew about my debut novel long before it ever made it to the printer. Everywhere I went, long lost friends were asking me when the book was coming out. This helped me to stay motivated because once everyone started asking me about the novel, I knew that I had to follow through with publishing the book

2.   Sending E-Mail Blasts

I collect mailing addresses and e-mail addresses from everyone that I meet. I've created a Microsoft Word and an e-mail database file on my computer to store names and personal addresses. Now, I do about one or two e-Blasts a week to everyone in my database regarding the status of sales, book signings, and future projects. Every time someone new is added to my system, I mail out an update to everyone. This keeps my book fresh in people's minds as they go about their daily lives. They'll be more inclined to talk about my book as they engage in leisurely conversations by the water cooler, at the gym, or at home.

You should also include a "signature" as a part of your e-mail address with your name, title, book cover, a link to your website, blog address, etc.

3. Developing a Website

Almost everyone has a webpage or a website these days, whether they're in business or not. Some people do it simply for the fun of it while others use it as a diverse marketing tool. Many publishers spend thousands of dollars on website development, then pay a monthly fee for someone to maintain and update it as needed. If there's a problem with the website, they have to wait for the computer technician to handle it.

Well, I didn't have the money or the time for that. I'm not a computer expert, but I can figure out a few things and follow good directions when necessary. So I found a low-cost website provider that offered a template, uploaded my information, and I routinely maintain it myself.

However, free websites are now available with some restrictions. They give you a free website in exchange for placing advertisements on the pages. You will still have to pay for a domain name and other premium upgrades. Check them out at:

- Freewebs.com

- Freewebsites.com

- Freewebsiteproviders.com

a. Choosing a Website Provider

I chose a website provider with 24/7 customer service and live on-line help for less than ten dollars a month. However, they required me to pay the entire fee up front at one time which was fine with me. You may contact them at:

Startlogic Inc.
919 E. Jefferson Street
Suite #100
Phoenix, AZ 85034
(800) 725-8064
Startlogic.com

Initially, I did have to get some assistance from a computer expert in order to maintain this website myself. However, now I'm completely self-sufficient when it comes to updating my pages. If I have a problem with anything, I simply call the toll free number for a quick resolution. My provider offers a 24/7 help line as well as on-line assistance.

Most websites come with e-mail accounts so that you may have multiple e-mail addresses to use. Be sure to include a signature line as a part of your messages with a link to your website. You should also include a graphic depiction of your book(s) as a marketing strategy. This way, people will become very familiar with your book cover and will be more likely to order it from you or pick up a copy once they see it in the bookstores.

Last but not least, be sure to set-up your website months prior to releasing your book so that you may start taking pre-orders. Yes, customers should be able to order your book as soon as they hear about it whether it's published or not. Once you have confirmed your publishing date, it's time to start collecting money. However, you must be able to deliver the goods on time because your customer will be looking for the product that you have promised to them.

b.   Accepting Credit Cards
If you want to accept credit cards via your website, you will have to contract with a company equipped to provide you with this service. I chose PayPal because they were recommended to me, and they have a very low commission rate.

They don't charge a set-up fee or a monthly fee for their services. They will accept the full payment, send me a message confirming that I have an order, and deposit the money into my PayPal account after taking out their small percentage. Check out their website for current rates and charges at:

PayPal.com
(402) 935-2050

You can go ahead and set-up your PayPal account now so that when your books arrive, you'll be ready to take orders immediately. You will not be charged a cent until someone orders your book. In fact, you can start advertising and taking pre-orders from your website before the book is even released. This method has worked well for some authors.

The first day that my book was released, they ran an article about me in the FAMUAN, the campus newspaper at Florida A & M University, and my account was activated that day. Once the deposit was made into my PayPal account, it only took a couple of days to transfer the funds to my business checking account.

4. Using Printed Materials

Printed materials such as bookmarks, brochures, business cards, flyers, postcards, and posters are a great way to promote your new books and business at a relatively low price. I ordered 2,500 postcards for my first book release. I mailed out a thousand to family, friends, and other locals. Then, whenever I received an order, I would send my new customer(s) several postcards to pass on to their circle of friends.

My postcards were size 4.25" x 6" which is the standard size. I used two different companies for printing my postcards. They both did a great job, and they had very fast turnaround services. You may reach these printers at:

a. **GotPrint.com**
   222 North Screenland Drive
   Burbank, CA 91505
   (818) 843-8888
   (818) 566-4082
   (877) 922-7374

b. **OvernightPrints.com**
   1800 East Garry Avenue
   Santa Ana, CA 92705
   (888) 677-2000

If you're interested in comparison shopping, you can do an Internet search at: **Postcards.com**

I only had a short synopsis and my website address on the back of my postcards. However, having the ISBN printed on the back will make it easier for the bookstores to locate your book in their database. If you also have the retail price printed on the back of the postcard, consumers will be prepared to pay that amount when they enter the bookstore.

Bookmarks are a good alternative to postcards and are less expensive to print. I haven't had any printed yet, but I am taking it under consideration. And, of course, business cards are very popular with publishers. I found a website where you can order 250 business cards for FREE. You simply pay for the shipping and handling cost. They may be reached at:

c.   **VistaPrint.com**
      100 Hayden Avenue
      Lexington MA 02421
      (800) 721-6214

Once you have written more than one book, brochures might be a better option for you. Instead of having two or three different postcards, you can showcase multiple books in one brochure and save on the printing cost of postcards. Make sure that you leave one panel blank in case you want to use them for mailing purposes.

In addition, I've used flyers and posters to promote local events such as book signings or workshops. It's an inexpensive way to help circulate your name in the community.

5.   Sending Press Releases
You should have a press release prepared for the day that your books arrive. Most of the local newspapers will not run these for independent publishers, but you should still ask them about it. (See the sample provided in the back of this book).

However, I did find an Internet website that posts press releases everyday for a low cost. You may contact them at:

PR Web International, Inc.
P. O. Box 333
 Alder Street
Ferndale, WA 98248
(866) 640-NEWS   24-hour editorial desk
PRWeb.com

This website will provide you with the guidelines for developing your copy. It will also offer tips for writing an effective press release, the proper format to use, and a template. However, some websites still offer free press releases with some restrictions at:

- PRfree.com
- PR.com
- Free-press-release.com

Be sure to keep copies of your press release for various uses. Whenever I mailed out letters or packages to bookstores, distributors, or book clubs, I always included a copy of my press release.

I also took part of the copy from my press release and had it made into a flyer for promotional appearances such as conferences and book festivals. I added a small picture of myself and the book cover. Then, I had it copied onto colored paper for added appeal.

6.   Sending Press Kits

Most bookstores and book clubs will ask you to send them a press kit (or media kit) along with a copy of your book for review. You should never just send a copy of your book without any promotional materials. Even when customers order your book, it's a good idea to include at least a business card or a brochure.

Here's a list of things that you may want to include in your kit:

- A picture of yourself
- A one-page biography
- Business cards
- Brochures showcasing your books
- Postcards
- A video or CD of your work
- Bookmarks
- Flyers
- Newspaper clippings of your work
- Interview transcripts from radio and/or television

7.   Contacting Newspapers, Radio, and Television Stations
You should use the local media to your advantage in marketing your book. There are several ways you can do this.

a.   Newspapers
Send the local newspapers a press release including book signing dates. If you're a college graduate, contact your alma mater's campus newspaper and request that they do an article about you.

I've been featured in the following newspapers:

1.   American Chronicle
2.   Capital Outlook
3.   Florida Courier
4.   The Famuan
5.   The Tallahassee Democrat

b.   Radio
I have made several talk radio show appearances locally, via the Internet, and via telephone. Make sure that you check out all of the options using this venue.

Radio is a great way to reach listeners all over the world without leaving your home. Here's the information for the first Internet radio interview that I did:

Artist First World Radio
1062 Parkside Drive
Alliance, OH 44601
(330) 823-2264
Artistfirst.com

Here's a few other Internet radio shows that you may want to check out for interviews:

- Letstalkhonestly.com
- Deloresthornton.com
- VoiceAmerica.com
- WTAL1450.com

c.   Television

Everyone wants to be on television, but it's very difficult to get those few minutes of fame. The local news stations would only interview non-profit organizations for their special shows. However, I was granted a 30-minute television interview with the FAMU campus broadcast station.

Be prepared to fax information to each company/organization, and give them a promotional copy of your book. Also, be sure to follow up with them.

8.   Contacting Colleges, Universities, and Libraries

You should contact your local community college and state university's Business, English, Reading, and Writing Departments. They may invite you to come in to speak with some of their classes and organizations around campus to help promote their literacy programs.

Administrators, professors, and instructors in these departments are always looking for ways to motivate their students to read and write, and you will be able to help them further their goals.

I have been to several community colleges, technical colleges, and universities to promote literacy along with encouraging students to read my books. It is my goal to give people an enjoyable story so that they will be encouraged to keep reading and keep buying new books especially in support of self-published authors.

In addition, I have had several book signings at the local libraries, and several of them have ordered my books. My first book signing was scheduled at one of the local branch libraries. They even helped me to promote the event by doing a poster and passing out postcards which really helped to spread the word.

The best thing about selling books to colleges, universities, and libraries is that that don't normally return books. Once a college or university has purchased your book, they'll keep it on the shelf until it's sold even if they have to reduce the price after several months or years. And a library will keep your book on the shelf until it's too raggedy to check out. So either way you look at it, it's a win-win situation for you.

For a complete listing of public libraries by state and their contact telephone numbers, please visit: **Publiclibraries.com**

9.   Contacting the Small Business Development Center
Your local Small Business Development Center (SBDC) may be willing to sponsor you for a workshop on writing or self-publishing. If you're interested in doing this, give them a call and politely offer your services to them. They may be happy to add you to the program list for one of their upcoming workshops or business conferences.

You will need to have a proposal prepared for your meeting with the director. Be sure to include an updated resume and a proposed workshop outline along with any pertinent facts regarding the sales progress of your book. Hopefully, if you've done this a few times before, it'll be easier when you approach them.

This is a wonderful opportunity for you to make connections with other business-minded people in your community. Just make sure that you are prepared to handle business.

You will probably be bombarded with questions during the workshop and you can meet with the individual participants after the official meeting time or set-up appointments for personalized conferences. You will have to determine the price that you wish to charge for conducting conferences and workshops. I recently began charging for my services as a workshop presenter and for private consulting. As an educator, I have enjoyed freely teaching people about the writing and publishing process. If profit is your only motive for writing, you may be sadly disappointed. I agree with Oprah Winfrey that you should do what you love, and the money will follow. I write and teach because it's absolutely what I love to do. Even if I hadn't sold a hundred books the first month, I'd still be writing.

10.   Contacting Book Clubs

Another way to market your book is through local and on-line book clubs. In my debut novel, I provided a special section labeled "Reading Group Questions" at the end for book club members. This was beneficial when I met with these organizations to discuss my book. The questions were already laid out by chapter and immediately pulled the members into a lively discussion.

When you contact the on-line book clubs, be sure to ask them about setting up a chat room with their members to discuss your work. You might even ask about doing a conference call for added fun. This will give them the opportunity to speak "live" with an author.

Most book clubs will be happy to give you a book review in exchange for a FREE copy of your work. Just be sure to follow-up with them after mailing your book in.

Here's a sampling of some of the on-line book clubs:

a.   African-American Literature Book Club
This is a popular website dedicated to black authors. They offer a registered listing of black book clubs.

> **AALBC**
> 55 West 116th Street, #195
> Harlem, NY 10026
> (866) 603-8394
> **Aalbc.com**

b.   Mosaic Books
This is an on-line bookstore with the largest listing of African-American book clubs on the Internet at:

> **Mosaicbooks.com/bookclubs.htm**

c.   RAWSISTAZ Book Club
The Reading and Writing Sistaz on-line book club has an awesome website dedicated to helping independent publishers. They also provide book reviews and post them on Amazon's website.

> **Rawsistaz Book Club**
> P. O. Box 1362
> Duluth, GA 30096
> (775) 363-8683
> (775) 416-4540
> **Rawsistaz.com**

d.   SORMAG Book Club
The Shades of Romance Magazine and book club is a wonderful site. They do book reviews and interviews on featured authors.

> **SORMAG.com**
> **SORMAG.blogspot.com**

e.   Circle of Friends Book Club I
This book club has fourteen chapters throughout the United States. However, the founding chapter is located in Valdosta, Georgia.

Cof1.com/cof1/chapters.html

f.   Avid-Readers

This is a website with a listing of African-American on-line book clubs. They provide web links to each site listed. In addition, they provide a list of new releases, upcoming releases, book reviews, and some information on self-publishing.

Avid-Readers.com

g.   Authors on Tour

This website provides a detailed directory of African-American book clubs in alphabetical order by states.

Authorsontour.com/bookclubs.htm

11.   Seeking Book Reviews

Book reviews are a great way to sell books, but they are very hard to come by especially in the major magazines. I have contacted several and they have all responded by saying that they don't review self-published books. But anyone can post a review for a book on Amazon. I encourage everyone who buys my titles to contact the on-line bookstore so that they may post reviews for my books on the Internet.

Another strategy that I used was to review many of the books that I had read so that I could leave my name on the author's review page with the title of my book printed. This way, my name was on several major authors' Amazon pages.

You may also send your book out to book clubs and other book reviewers for their feedback or blurbs to post on your website or the back of future book releases. Most of them will request that you send a printed copy of the book but some of them will accept an electronic copy (PDF) for review. Therefore, you can save on the printing cost of the book as well as postage, so be sure to ask if a PDF is acceptable.

Here's a list of a few places that have done book reviews for me:

- APOOO.org
- Blackbutterflyreview.com
- Book-remarks.com
- B-Zine.com
- CBBooksdistribution.com
- Ebonyfly.com
- Journalofcolor.com
- Letstalkhonestly.com
- Maemwg3@yahoo.com
- OOSAonlinebookclub.com
- Rawsistaz.com
- Sisterdivasmagazine.com
- Sormag.com
- Theromancereadersconnection.com
- Urban-reviews.com

12.   Attending Book Fairs

Most major bookstores like Barnes & Noble's host some type of book fair or book expo during the year to highlight local authors. These events are usually hosted by the writers' group in that particular city. So if you haven't joined a writing association in your area, you should check with them to see if anything has been organized.

Book Fairs are a great way to bring local authors together and introduce them to the community as well as each other. The independent and the major bookstores are normally very supportive of these types of events because of the community involvement.

13.   Scheduling Book Signings and Conferences

You want to schedule as many book signings as you can. Then, be sure to spread the word by mailing out invitations or flyers, or by sending e-mails to everyone on your list and asking them to forward the announcement to their "e-mail buddies."

Then, you should plan to attend conferences where you can be the keynote speaker or conduct a workshop on writing and self-publishing. So far, I have traveled to several states for business conferences and presented free workshops on self-publishing. However, I'm able to sell books after each event as compensation.

In order to reduce your traveling expenses, you should visit places where you have people that you can stay with or have a group to sponsor you. I'm a strong believer in the saying, "Where there's a will, there's a way." If you're a determined and motivated person, you're already on the road to success.

On-line conferences have grown in popularity. I recently participated in one organized by Shades of Romance magazine and conducted a workshop on "Self Publishing." Participants were able to post comments and ask questions directly from the website on a daily basis.

14.   Trying Business Partners

Another option that you may wish to consider is taking on limited-time business partners to sell your book(s). Essentially, these individuals will serve as vendors for your product and you will pay them a flat fee or a percentage from every book that they sell within a specific time-frame.

Be sure to draw up some type of contract for them to sign and make sure that it's reviewed by an attorney before anyone signs. You want to be sure that you're protected as well as your business partners.

This is a great way to gain free publicity for your books and your business. Now that others have a vested interested in your products, the word will spread even faster. And, of course, that can only work to your advantage.

15.   Blogging on the Internet

I've been reading about blogging in the writing magazines for the last couple of years. It's taken me that long to figure it out.

But now that I've started blogging, I think that it's a great way to promote yourself and your books.

Blogging is simply a way of journaling on the Internet for free. You can write about any subject that you like, and instantly publish it on the Internet. Then, others can read your thoughts and post their comments regarding whatever it is that you posted.

Blog Tours have become very popular in recent years. It works just like a regular book tour, but you're hosted on different blog sites by various authors or fans. It's a great way to gain exposure without leaving the comfort of your home.

You can read my current blogs at:

http://Blog.myspace.com/Barbarajoewilliams

16. Building an Authors' Network

Once your book is published, it's a good idea to start building a network of authors to help you promote your work. In return, you should also be willing to help them by hosting book signings together, reading each other's work for feedback, and providing blurbs for upcoming books.

It's especially good to network with other local authors just to keep apprised of literary events taking place in your area. I've learned that there is strength in numbers. By that I mean that readers are more likely to come out to see a group of authors than they are to come out to see a single author that they've never heard of.

So by simply having a group of writers, you're more likely to increase your chances of the local community knowing someone that's included in the affair. Think about it.

I was surprised at the number of local authors in my city once I started seeking them out while promoting my books. Now, I plan to host at least one event a year to bring them all together for a day of community-based fun and exposure.

There's nothing like having a network of people that can identify and support you as an author and a publisher. If you're not sure about how to find authors in your community, visit the bookstore and ask if they have a section specifically for local authors.

17. Publishing Other Authors

Another great way to promote yourself as an author and publisher is to publish other authors. Now that you have some publishing experience under your belt, you may want to venture out and help someone else along their publishing journey.

In return, they're helping you by promoting your business whenever they sell their own books. It's also a wonderful feeling to know that I've helped someone else to fulfill their lifelong dream of becoming a published writer.

18. Participating in an Anthology

Being a part of an anthology is a terrific way to increase your notability. If you're in a book with ten other authors, then each of you will probably reach a different audience or segment of people than you normally would. Therefore, it'll provide even more publicity for you and your publishing business.

19. Sponsoring Writing Contests

Sponsoring a writing contest is another great way to generate free publicity for your book company. Aspiring authors will jump at the opportunity to enter, especially if the award-winning prize is to be published in an anthology with you.

I tried this strategy and I ended up with seventeen winners who all received a free publishing credit in the anthology titled, *How I Met My Sweetheart*, a collection of short inspirational love stories.

Automatically, I had seventeen authors promoting a book that I was also a part of creating. They were excited about the adventure and so was I. We were able to create an amazing amount of publicity for our unique project.

20.   Becoming a Book Reviewer

That's right! Maybe you should consider becoming a book reviewer for an on-line magazine or your local newspaper. They don't usually pay a lot but at least you'll receive free books and publicity on a continuing basis.

21.   Writing Magazine Articles

Now that you have a publishing credit, you should consider submitting articles to various magazines or monthly publications. It's a great way to establish yourself as a literary entrepreneur.

It's great to see your work on the bookstore shelves. However, selling on your own can prove to be much more profitable.

22.   Starting Your Own E-Newsletter

Creating your own monthly e-newsletter or e-zine to share with your on-line friends is another way to keep in touch with your readers and share literary information with them. You can easily set-up a newsletter template using software located on the Internet.

23.   Joining a Webring

A webring is a circle of links to other websites from your website. And each time that someone clicks on the webring link, they'll go to another website until they eventually return back to yours. It's one of the least expensive ways that I know of to advertise your book/business on the Internet.

24.   Adding Contact Links

Adding a page of contact links on your website is another way to promote your book/business and to keep customers coming back to you. Simply exchange links with other authors, then keep your contact page updated and your customers will keep returning to it for valuable information.

If you visit my website, you'll find an entire page dedicated to links directing you to other websites belonging to authors, book clubs, book reviewers, etc.

25. Setting a Book Release Date

Setting your book release date around a family reunion, holiday, or significant event will greatly increase your chances of selling lots of books. Most of your family members will be happy to know that you've published your first book. So the next time that you have a family reunion, you should have hundreds of copies ready to sell. Think about it; you'll have family coming to the reunion from all over the world, and they should be taking several copies of your book back home with them.

Essentially, you'll have your own distribution center via your family members. And they'll be so proud of you that they'll tell all of their friends about their relative's book.

Then the next month, you should receive orders for hundreds more books because everybody wants to know somebody who knows somebody who wrote a book.

People do more shopping for books and other items during holidays. Christmas is not the only holiday in America. For instance, Valentine's Day would be a great time to release a romance novel or a relationship book.

If you're writing a book about college, then early August would be an ideal time to set the release date. And, of course, if you're writing a book set around Christmastime, then it should be released in November or December versus May or June. Think about local events in your town that people like to celebrate, and plan your book release date in time for it. If your family reunion is scheduled for June that would be the ideal time to have your very first book signing while you have everyone together.

26. Contacting Specialty Stores

If you're writing a book about animals, then you should try to get it carried in the pet shops. If you're writing a book about hair care, or one that has a hairdresser as a main character, then you should try to sell it in the local hair salons. Try to think of different ways to reach your target audience.

27.   Joining a Writing Association

This will help you create a bond with published and unpublished authors as well as showcase your work. Most writing associations have a website with a link to the author's webpage. In addition, they may host an annual conference or workshop which will give you another opportunity to display your talents.

I'm a current member of Tallahassee Writers' Association. They've been very supportive of my local booking events.

28.   Creating an Order Form

Place an order form in the back of your book to make it convenient for the reader to order more copies of your work. Be sure to include your mailing address, telephone number, price of book, and shipping costs.

29.   Advertising in Your Book

Placing an advertisement in the back of your current book for future releases is a good marketing strategy. Include a short synopsis of your work along with your personal contact information and ISBNs for all books.

30.   Placing Cards in Mail-Outs

Use your business card as a way to advertise in mail-outs. Simply place a couple of business cards in your Christmas greeting cards, bill payment envelopes, drive-thru window envelopes at the bank, etc. If you place them in greeting cards during the holidays, your cards and mailing costs are both tax deductible.

31.   Donating Books

Yes, you'll have to giveaway a few books to help promote your work. Don't worry; they're all tax deductible as promotional items. Be sure to donate at least one copy to your local library and then encourage them to order more later on. You may also want to create a gift basket including your book(s) for charity events in your neighborhood.

32. Carrying Your Book with You

Always have a copy of your book on you or in your car while you're shopping or running errands. You never know who you're going to meet in the grocery store that might be interested in buying or just seeing a copy of your new book. Be prepared to take advantage of every promotional opportunity that you have.

If you're standing in line at the post office, have a copy of your book in your hand and strike up a conversation with the person behind or in front of you. They'll be thrilled to know that you're the author of the book that you're holding.

33. Pursuing International Markets

You may want to look into selling your books to international markets especially if you're from another country or island. This is an idea that you can discuss with your distributor or explore on your own. Sometimes books, just like music, tend to do better overseas than they do in America. So it's something that's worth looking into.

34. Using Your Vehicle

Here's another promotion strategy that you might want to consider. You can have your book cover painted on the side of your vehicle or have a removable sign made to post in the rear window. Be sure to include your website and ordering information on the sign.

35. Teaching On-line Classes

Now that you've published your book, it's time to teach others how to do the same thing. Search for on-line educational institutions or professional organizations and offer them your services. It's free publicity and money in your account.

36. Thinking Outside the Box

Keep thinking of non-traditional ways to sell your product. Remember, the majority of printed books are not sold in bookstores. It's up to you, the author, to do your best to promote and sell your book using as many avenues as possible. You must "think outside the box."

That's it! You've completed the course! These are the basic elements that you need to become a successful self-published author.

I'm sure that you'll learn even more as you actually proceed through the various steps. I just hope that this has better prepared you for your publishing journey.

Hopefully, this ten-step program will change your life. There will never be a better time than right now to start making your publishing dreams come true.

If you're ready to take the next step towards self-publishing, I wish you the best of luck. Maybe I'll see you at a book signing someday, or better yet, maybe we'll have one together. Just keep me informed of your progress.

I'm ready to realize my dreams for self-publishing. _____

I already have marketing strategies in place. _____

My marketing plan is to use the following techniques:

1._____

2._____

3._____

4._____

5._____

6._____

CHECKLIST AFTER PRINTING
(Sample)

_____ Inventory your shipment

_____ Check for a packing list

_____ Store books in a clean dry place

_____ Mail promotional items (postcards, etc.)

_____ Set-up book signings & calendar

_____ Write a press release

_____ Notify local media regarding signings

_____ Set-up publishing workshops

_____ E-mail on-line contacts

_____ Mail-out promotional copies for review

_____ Contact book distributors

_____ Contact local & major bookstores

_____ Contact the local library

_____ Schedule workshops on self-publishing

_____ Contact on-line bookstores and book clubs

_____ Get mentally ready to promote your book

CHECKLIST BEFORE PRINTING
(Sample)

_____ Complete manuscript

_____ Get manuscript edited

_____ Send for copyright

_____ Research your title at Amazon.com and Copyright.gov

_____ Register your company name

_____ Apply for city & county license

_____ Develop a marketing plan

_____ Order ISBN

_____ Buy office supplies

_____ Get printing specifications for your book

_____ Draft a book cover copy

_____ Contact the Library of Congress

_____ Choose a printer

_____ Set the release date for your book

_____ Set-up a storage area

_____ Order postcards and promotional materials

Barbara Joe-Williams

MISTAKES FIRST TIME AUTHORS MAKE (25)
-How to Avoid Them-

As a first time self-published author, you want to avoid making as many costly mistakes as possible. Based on research and several years of publishing experience, I'd like to share some of the mistakes that I've made and show you how to avoid making them. Please proceed with caution.

1) Publishing books with unattractive covers and spending too much money on them. Hire someone to design an attractive front book cover. Or you can save money by developing the book cover drafts yourself. Simply download royalty-free pictures and add your own text.

2) Printing books in large quantities because it's the most economical value. With print-on-demand (POD) printers, you no longer have to print large quantities of books to receive a good return on your investment. You can print as few or as many as you need at one time.

3) Paying large amounts for website development and maintenance. Find a web hosting company, download a template, upload your book information, and maintain the site yourself for a low monthly or yearly fee. Most of these companies provide 24/7 customer support.

4) Working without an action plan or any means of accountability. Writing may be your passion, but publishing is a business. Therefore, you have to develop a business plan to follow and show accountability for your funds.

5) Not testing the cover design or the titles before publishing. The key to avoiding this mistake is developing more than one book cover draft and testing them on potential buyers. You can also develop more than one title and test them, too.

6) Waiting until the book is published to start marketing it. Start marketing your book the first day that you start writing it. Tell everyone that you know and/or meet about your new project.

7) Pricing the book too high or too low based on the market. Be sure to research the price of other books on the market that are similar to yours and price your book accordingly.

8) Not identifying the target market for the publication. The first rule of publishing is to know your target market and how to reach them. Where do they live and shop? How will they learn about your book?

9) Not pre-selling copies of the book or taking pre-orders. You can set-up your website to take credit cards and start taking pre-orders months before the book is ever printed.

10) Relying solely on one marketing model to sell the book. Develop several marketing strategies before your book is published. Communicate with other authors to find out what has and hasn't worked for them.

11) Writing books you think people should read instead of what the market demands. The publishing business is also a matter of supply and demand. You may enjoy writing fiction, but a non-fiction project that serves a desire or need will be more profitable.

12) Paying for expensive advertising, marketing/promotional ideas. Marketing doesn't have to be an expensive venture. Look for strategies that will provide you with free publicity such as library workshops and radio interviews.

13) Writing the book without developing a timeline for completion. Once you start writing your book, set some realistic goals for completing it and stick to it. Don't let down your target market after you've announced the book to them.

14) Not having a reader's or audience database. You can start developing a reader's database as soon as you start working on your book by contacting local book club members and attending library events.

15) Not being open to the editing or revising process. Find an editor that you feel comfortable with and trust. This will make it easier to accept criticism and make recommended revisions.

16) Missing deadlines for writing and publishing. It's very important to the success of your writing career that you meet the realistic deadlines that you've already set. Once you set a book release date, readers will be expecting the book at that time.

17) Not reading enough from the competition. Make sure you know what the competition has to offer and be able to explain how your book is different. You want your project to stand out from every other book on your chosen subject.

18) Wasting time trying to make the copy perfect the first time. Focus on completing the manuscript and getting it to the editor instead of trying to make sure that it's perfect. You'll have plenty of time to go back and make revisions later.

19) Not being able to verbalize the content of the book in a concise manner. You should be able to summarize your entire manuscript in a few sentences upon request. Most readers want to know what the heart of the book is about in one-minute or less.

20) Not joining a writer's group or reading magazines, or attending conferences for writers. Joining a writer's group is a way to learn from other authors or aspiring authors. Reading *Writer's Digest* each month will provide you with valuable information and attending conferences will give you an opportunity to meet major publishers and agents.

21) Relying solely on bookstores to sell the books to make a profit. According to the Publisher's Marketing Association, approximately 52 percent of published books are <u>not</u> sold in bookstores. This means that you must find more creative ways of selling your product.

22) Concentrating too much on sales and not enough on publicity. Of course, your publishing goal is to make money, but some events should just be about publicity and then the money will follow.

23) Not reinvesting money back into your book business. This is a valuable lesson to learn. If you spend all your profits on personal expenses, it's impossible to keep producing books to keep your business growing.

24) Sending in for a copyright before the manuscript has been edited. You should wait until your manuscript has been completely edited before sending in the copyright registration. Once you make significant changes to the manuscript, the copyright certificate is no longer valid.

25) Not asking for help when needed. Self-publishing doesn't mean that you have to do everything yourself. Hire others to do the technical things that you may not understand or have the time to properly address.

RESOURCE GUIDE for WRITERS

Other book and magazine resources available on self-publishing and writing:

1.   **Authorsden.com**

2.   **Bibookreview.com**
      Black Issues Book Review Magazine

3.   **Bookingmatters.com**
      Booking Matters Magazine

4.   **Booksjustbooks.com**

5.   **Guide to Book Publishers, Editors, and Literary Agents,** Jeff Herman

6.   **Handbook for Writers**, Leggett, Mead & Charvat

7.   **How to Self-Publish that Great Novel**
      Delores Thornton

8.   **Pma-online.org**
      Publishers Marketing Association

9.   **Selfpublishedauthors.com**

10.   **Selfpublishing.com**

11.   **Selfpublishingbasics.com**

12.   **Selfpublishingworkshop.com**
      A FREE online e-course

13. **The African-American Guide to Successful Self-Publishing**, Powell & Debose

14. **The African-American Guide to Writing and Publishing Nonfiction**, Jewell Parker Rhodes

15. **The African-American Writer's Handbook**, Robert Fleming

16. **The Self-Publishing Manual**, Dan Poynter

17. **Writersdigest.com**
Writer's Digest Magazine

18. **Writers.net**

19. **Writersmarket.com**

20. **Writer's Market**, Kathryn S. Brogan

21. **Writers on Writing-Volume II**, Jane Smiley

22. **Writing Romance**, Vanessa Grant

23. **Writing the Breakout Novel**, Donald Maass

SAMPLE-BOOKSTORE-LETTER

(Current date)

Barnes & Noble Bookstore
Small Press Department
122 5th Avenue
New York, NY 10011

ATTENTION: Small Press Department

Amani Publishing has been in operation for over a year now and recently released an inspiring fictional romance novel titled, ***Forgive Us This Day***, in late November. *Forgive Us This Day* is a love story focusing on the faith, hope, and real love shared between two African-American married people set in the urban city of Jacksonville, Florida. It's a different type of romance novel that's told from a Christian as well as a secular perspective. This book is also the first product of a three part series scheduled to be published by this debut author within the next two years.

Forgive Us This Day has been well received and reviewed by several on-line book clubs. It recently received a five star rating from Tanya Bates, a reviewer, for C & B Books in New York. I've hosted local book signings, and I have signings scheduled in two other states so far. In addition, I have been asked to be the guest speaker for two business functions and plan to host a workshop on self-publishing in May. I'm also a motivational speaker who has been visiting colleges and university classes to promote literacy along with my book.

The novel is currently being marketed through postcards, my website address at: www.Barbarajoewilliams.com, and with two of the local book stores as well as being carried by the local library. I have a vendor account with Barnes & Noble's College Bookstores. In addition, the title was recently approved for back ordering through Baker & Taylor book distributors. The retail price is $13.95 (ISBN 0-9752851-0-6). You may reach me during business hours at: (850) 264-3341 cell, (850) 877-7348 home, or (850) 878-1006 fax, or e-mail me at: Amanipublishing@aol.com.

Thank you for your time and consideration. I am enclosing a copy of my book and promotional postcards along with the Internet press release. Please give me an opportunity to work with the Barnes & Noble trade stores in conjunction with the college book stores.

Literally yours,

Barbara Joe-Williams

SAMPLE-DISTRIBUTOR-LETTER

(Current date)

American Wholesale Book Co.
131 S. 25th Street
Irondale, AL 35210

ATTENTION: New Acquisitions

I would like to introduce you to Barbara Joe-Williams, owner of Amani Publishing, located in Tallahassee, Florida. However, I was born and raised in Rosston, Arkansas, and served four years in the United States Navy prior to attending college. I am a graduate of Tallahassee Community College and Florida A & M University. As a former business school teacher and guidance counselor who happens to be an avid reader, I decided to become a self-made publisher. After two years of working as a Reading Assistant at the community college, I was inspired to follow my dream of writing and publishing my own book.

Amani Publishing has been in operation for almost a year and just recently released an inspiring fictional romance novel titled, ***Forgive Us This Day***, in late November. *Forgive Us This Day* is a love story focusing on the faith, hope, and real love shared between two African-American married people. This book is the first product of a three part series scheduled to be published by this debut author within the next two years.

The book is currently being marketed and promoted via my website address at: www.barbarajoewilliams.com, and with one of the local book stores as well as being carried by the local library. The retail price is $13.95 (ISBN 0-9752851-0-6). You may reach me at: (850) 264-3341 cell, (850) 877-7348 home, or (850) 878-1006 fax, or e-mail me at: Amanipublishing@aol.com.

Thank you for your time and consideration. I am enclosing a copy of my book along with a self-addressed stamped postcard. I look forward to hearing from you soon.

Literally yours,

Barbara Joe-Williams

SAMPLE-PRESS-RELEASE

FOR IMMEDIATE RELEASE:

Debut Novelist Writes an Inspiring Love Story

The new fictional romance novel staged in the urban city of Jacksonville, Florida, centers on the trials and tribulations of an African-American married couple.

Tallahassee, FL (PRWEB) (Current date) — *Forgive Us This Day* is an inspiring love story focusing on the faith, hope, and real love shared between two married people. According to The Divorce Center statistics, 2.2 million couples married and 1.1 million couples divorced in 1998. In 2000, 58 million couples were married, yet separated. People between the ages of 25 – 39 make up 60% of all divorces and over one million children are affected by divorce each year. Divorce Magazine reported in 2002, that only 52 percent of married people reach their fifteenth anniversary, and in 1994, Florida was rated as one of the ten highest divorce states.

Despite these statistics, the author wants to show readers that African-American married couples can be romantic, face difficulties, and persevere through adversity together. Written with Jacksonville, Florida, as the backdrop of the story, this couple learns a lesson in love as well as forgiving the ultimate act of betrayal. The two main characters of the new romance novel, *Forgive Us This Day*, Alese and Michael Wayne, are a loving thirty-something couple who have been married for fifteen years and are in the process of adopting a two-year old daughter when tragedy strikes. Alese, a strong willed woman, learns that there is a problem with the adoption and receives a note that her husband is having an affair with one of his employees on the same day that her mother suffers a heart attack. They have forgiven each other for lesser offenses many times before, but will they both be forgiven for this day?

Barbara Joe-Williams, author of the new novel, is a graduate of Tallahassee Community College and Florida A&M University. She has enjoyed reading romance novels all of her adult life. She has been married for twenty-three years and has a four-year old daughter. She is a former business school teacher and guidance counselor who is currently working as a full-time publisher and writer. Being a self-published author is a daring adventure, but it's working well for her. She has already started her second novel to be released in November 2005.

"I enjoy reading love stories centering on married couples with positive African American men. Unfortunately, most romance novels focus on single people in their twenties trying to make a love connection. Although I read a lot of those books, I decided to write the type of story that would also appeal to my age group. Hopefully, whether you're single, engaged, married, or divorced, you'll be inspired to read this sensuous novel about faith, hope, and real love."

Book statistics:
Genre, Romance
ISBN, 0975285106
Price, $13.95

ABOUT THE AUTHOR

Barbara Joe-Williams is a freelance author and an independent publisher living in Tallahassee, Florida. As the owner of Amani Publishing, she has also published several non-fiction books for other aspiring authors.

Her books may be ordered from her website, online bookstores, or from retail bookstores:

How I Met My Sweetheart Anthology, February 2007
ISBN: 097528519X

Falling for Lies, October 2006
ISBN: 0975285130

Dancing with Temptation, November 2005
ISBN: 0975285122

Forgive Us This Day, November 2004
ISBN: 0975285106

You may contact Barbara at:
AmaniPublishing.net or
AmaniPublishing@aol.com

ACKNOWLEDGEMENTS

I want to thank all of the many people who purchased my novels and encouraged me to write this handbook for others interested in writing, self-publishing, and marketing.

I have to personally thank my husband, Wilbert, for supporting me with my writing efforts and for doing the laundry while I was writing this manuscript.

To my daughter, Amani, thanks for helping your mommy sell books. Maybe someday I'll be able to return the favor.

To my family and friends, God bless each and every one of you for your prayers and words of encouragement. I have become much stronger because of you all.

To the bookstores and the book clubs that are supporting my titles, thanks for taking a chance on me.

I want to thank Donna Austin, Doris Maloy, Rhonda Mattox, and Judy Williams for their quotations at the front of the book. You all have been more than inspirational to me.

Thanks to Jessica Wallace, my editor, for her expertise and friendship. We have become a great team. I'm looking forward to the next project with you.

<u>Notes</u>

<u>Notes</u>

<u>Notes</u>

Barbara Joe-Williams

[AP] ORDER FORM

To order additional copies of, **A Writer's Guide to Self-Publishing and Marketing**, complete the form below.

Mail to: **Amani Publishing**
                        P. O. Box 12045
                        Tallahassee, FL 32317
                        (850)-264-3341

E-mail: **AmaniPublishing@aol.com**

Website: **www.AmaniPublishing.net**

Name_____

Address_____

City_____State_____

E-mail address_____

Telephone (home)_____

Telephone (cell)_____

I am enclosing $15.00 per book for _____books
(Includes tax and shipping)

Total enclosed $_____

Thank you for your order!

Printed in the United States
126429LV00004B/14/P